Hearing God's Voice from Within

Hearing God's Voice from Within

Mickey Bonner

ISBN 1-878578-17-0
Copyright © 1998 by Mickey Bonner
All Rights Reserved
Published by Mickey Bonner Evangelistic Association
PO Box 680368, Houston, Texas 77268-0368
Printed in the United States of America

Dedication

This writing is gratefully dedicated to the Fincher family whom God in His providence raised up to stand with this work.

To Fred Fincher—a man of great faith and ability to believe God. His constant praying for us kept us anointed. He is now in the presence of Jesus Christ. I will miss him.

And to his wife Pearl who deeply loves the Lord, and to her children and their families who have also become close friends to me, my wife and our ministry; Don, Patricia, Andy, Fred Jr., Roger, John, Butch, Teresa, and Vicki.

I thank God for the fruit of righteousness that comes from a lifestyle and example. Such is this family.

Devotedly,

Mickey Bonner

Other Books by Mickey Bonner

Brokenness, the Forgotten Factor of Prayer
Brokenness, Study Guide
Spiritual Warfare Prayer Study Guide
God Can Heal Your Mind
Prayer is Warfare
The Scriptural Way to Get Out of Debt
God's Answer to the Critical Christian—KYMS
Deliverance the Children's Bread
Spiritual Warfare Manual
What's Wrong With America: Satan's Attack on the Home
Spiritual Warfare Syllabus
The Christian Home Syllabus

For a catalog of Dr. Bonner's other materials write:
MBEA
PO Box 680368
Houston, Texas 77268-0368
Phone: 1-800-365-7729
Fax: 1-218-580-0175
Our Website is http://mbea.org
Email - mbea@mbea.org

Acknowledgments

I would like to thank the following people that gave assistance in bringing this book to print. The Lord used them mightily throughout this project.

Dr. H.D. McCarty
Pastor Duane Roach
Ted Shadid
Matt and Sally Montgomery
Lee Fredrickson
Mickey II and Becky Bonner

My wife Margaret, my wonderful companion whom I love dearly more every day.

I would also like to thank all those that have prayed continually for me and this ministry.

And, Foremost, to Jesus Christ who has become more real to me in every way. I praise Him for His wondrous, glorious presence in my life.

Table of Contents

Foreword

Success is the progressive realization of the will of God for any life. This success may not seem successful in the eyes of a secular society.

Contrariwise, failure is being successful in that which is not God's will. Such success is failure even though in the eyes of many it may seem to be ultimate success.

It has been wisely stated that nothing lies outside the possibility of answered prayer except that which lies outside the will of God. How important it is, therefore, that we know clearly God's will. God's will is not something we find. In the truest analysis, the will of God finds us as we surrender, trust, and obey.

The will of God is not something grievous, though it may sometimes be rigorous. The will of God, according to Romans 12:1-2, is good, perfect, and acceptable. It is really what we, ourselves, would choose for ourselves if we had enough sense to choose it.

Indeed, we may choose that which is outside God's will. We are free to choose as we wish, but we are not free to choose the consequences of our choice.

Mickey Bonner, through a lifetime of study and prayer, was anointed to write this volume. My prayer is that the reader will find for himself the pleasure and joy that come by discovering and doing God's will. How wonderful it is when we do that which a loving God created us and redeemed us to do—His perfect will.

Adrian Rogers
Pastor of Bellevue Baptist Church, and
Love Worth Finding Ministries
Memphis, Tennessee.

The will of God is the mind of Christ acting within and through the believer at the level of His conscious understanding. The only way to hear consistently from the Great Shepherd is by the constant pursuit of Christ. You must stay close to the Shepherd. In studying the Word, you find that God is light. As you abandon yourself to Him, you will discover that in you, this light travels a pre-planned path as the daily will of God is worked out in your life.

— Mickey Bonner

Chapter One

How to Find the Will of God

I beseech you therefore, brethren, by the mercies of God, that ye present your bodies a living sacrifice, holy, acceptable unto God, which is your reasonable service. And be not conformed to this world: but be ye transformed by the renewing of your mind, that ye may prove what is that good, and acceptable, and perfect, will of God (Romans 12:1-2).

In this day of busy religious life, a few people have become weary in well doing. These Christians are caught up in the busyness of "good works." The Holy Spirit within brings them to the place of realizing there is something deeper to the spiritual life than promotion, emotion, or commotion—and there is. As they hunger for God's direction, they realize satan has trapped them into Christian doing in place of spiritual being. "Doing" is man's concept of the Christian life. "Being" is God performing His will through the Christian's life. My purpose in writing this book is to show believers Christianity is far more than physical activity. Those who choose to grow will become aware that God has made His perfect will available for their lives. It is there for the yielding. You might say there is a whole new world out there just for the asking. So, "ask and you shall receive" God's perfect will for your life.

The only person who will ever find the active will of God is the Christian who is truly seeking and yielding totally to Christ. Only he will know God's true purpose and plan. This individual will minister by the mind and power of God, rather than in the effort of the flesh. To come to this abundant state of being, one must absolutely abandon himself in total surrender to Jesus Christ. In doing so, he will begin to be sensitive to the person of the Holy Spirit within. By wholly committing to God, he will begin to hear intuitively the voice of the Holy Spirit. He will then become responsive to the Spirit's leading, teaching and direction for his life. What an incredible place to be!

You say, "How do I begin to find the will of the Lord for my life?" The Scriptures tell us we must love Him with all of our hearts if we are to find God's will. Our lives must be totally His; for God says, *"My sheep hear My voice."* When the Shepherd starts in a new direction, the sheep knows his Master's voice, and follows Him. From this place of obedience, he becomes sensitive first to hearing and then to obeying. You must understand, the Shepherd extends His ministry through the sheep. Never will the Shepherd follow a sheep except to chasten and restore it to the flock (Hebrews 12:5-8).

Sheep must follow the Shepherd

Many years ago I read a story about a shepherd and a passerby. In their encounter, the stranger noticed a sheep with a splint on its leg. The sheep lay closest to the shepherd as the flock bedded down for the night. The stranger asked if the sheep had fallen from a ledge. The shepherd replied, "No. I broke his leg with my staff." He went on to explain that this particular sheep had a habit of wandering away from the flock. To stop this, he took his staff and broke its leg. The sheep, unable to feed himself, had to be fed by the shepherd. He stated, "At first, he would bite at my hand, but soon he began to lick my hand and receive his food from me. Now, he stays constantly by my side." I remember the lesson of this story as I look back at my experience as a Christian wandering from God's will. Oh, how many times He has broken me to keep me close to Him. I am so grateful that He has, and does.

The only way to hear consistently from the Great Shepherd is by the constant pursuit of Christ. You must stay close to the Shepherd. In studying the Word, you find that God is light. As you abandon yourself to Him, you will discover that in you, this light travels a pre-planned path as the daily will of God is worked out in your life.

> **Wherefore, my beloved, as ye have always obeyed, not as in my presence only, but now much more in my absence, work out your own salvation with fear and trembling (Phil. 2:12).**

The Scriptures also tell us:

> **For we are God's (own) Handiwork (His workmanship), recreated in Christ Jesus, (born anew) that we may do those good works which God predestined (planned beforehand) for us, (taking paths which He prepared ahead of time) that we should walk in them [living the good life which He prearranged and made ready for us to live] (Ephesians 2:10 Amplified).**

The Christian's part is constantly to keep up with the light by going after Christ with his whole heart. When you do this, God unfolds His will in your life by the process of metamorphosis. This is the Greek word for "transformed" in Romans 12:2. The dictionary describes "metamorphosis" as a "change of physical form, structure, or substance, especially by supernatural means." This change unfolds as a believer seeks God over a period of time.

This marvelous change comes only to the person who is pursuing Jesus constantly. If the child of God, however, is not willing to lay down his life and "take up his cross," he will never know the constant active will of God. He will be like the overwhelming majority of baby Christians who say, "I have no idea what God's will is for my life." On other occasions, he will say, "What do you mean God speaks to you? He never speaks to me." He operates by reason, not revelation; by words, not wisdom. He lives by principles laid out by men rather than experiencing the Person of Christ within. There is no real peace, joy, or victory. He lives under his circumstances instead of living above them. He reads the Word but is *"dull of hearing,"* never receiving from the Holy Spirit *"truth in the inward parts."*

Again, God's personal will comes by revelation, not by reason or religious activity. God commands us to *"walk in the Spirit."* When the Shepherd starts for another location, He speaks and the sheep begin to move as they keep their eyes constantly upon Him. Religion is satan's strategy to divert you from God. He wants you to revolve your life around a certain set of standards, rules, doctrines and programs. In your sincerity you actively participate as best you can, when you can. Then, when you labor faithfully in a denomination or group, you are a called a "good Christian" according to their standards.

Satan sets up his religious course using human patterns of activity. God sets the life of Christ to be our life.

> **When Christ, [who is] our life, shall appear, then shall ye also appear with him in glory (Colossians 3:4).**

By and through Him alone God accomplishes His personal will through us. Satan turns the individual's natural search for truth into confusion. He diverts attention from the only true way by substituting religious activity and orthodox creeds for the truth. Because of this, there are over 20,000 Christian denominations, all claiming to get their "truth" from the Bible. As a result a Christian does the will of God as he conceives it, not as he receives it. The Christian constantly faces the decision of who and what is right by his own reasoning. Satan authors this style of Christianity and through it has birthed the thousands of religions that keep men from truly worshipping God. Philippians 3:3 explains the word *"worship"* by stating we worship Him in the Spirit and by the Spirit.

For we [Christians] are the true circumcision, who worship God in spirit and by the Spirit of God and exult and glory and pride ourselves in Jesus Christ, and put no confidence or dependence [on what we are] in the flesh and on outward privileges and physical advantages and external appearances (Philippians 3:3 Amplified).

No one can truly worship or walk with God except by the Holy Spirit.

Busy, Busy, Busy

Some years ago, a man wrote a book titled *Building a Standard Sunday School.* That well-written book offers many practical how-tos designed to bring people into the church to hear the Gospel. The author outlines various ways for Christians to bring people into the church through physical effort. Let me say, I believe the man who wrote the book was led of the Lord to do so. Evidently Sunday School has been the place for new birth and spiritual growth for multitudes through the years. Also, I must say here that I have nothing against building church attendance. However, I believe we must operate from the drive of the Spirit rather than out of the works of the flesh.

When God's Spirit falls in supernatural revival, there is no room to seat all who come. Revival is the result of Christians being consumed and motivated by the Holy Spirit's presence. Through the experience come eternal results. There are those, however, who work themselves to death because they think physical activity is the evidence of the Holy Spirit's control. Physical activity—or what the Scriptures call "works"—has been carried over into Christendom as the proof of the Spirit's control. Satan has so promoted this concept that many even believe they must do something physically religious to pay penance for sins committed. This is not so. Christ's life extended through His children procures the outworking of God's will.

Some years ago, a song was written that expresses well this position. It's title is *Follow Me*.

One verse says:
> I work so hard for Jesus
> I often boast and say
> I've sacrificed a lot of things
> To walk the narrow way.
>
> I gave up fame and fortune
> I'm worth a lot to Thee
> Then I heard Him
> Gently say to me
>
> I left the throne in glory
> And counted it but loss
> My hands were nailed in anger
> Upon the cruel cross
>
> But now we'll make the journey
> With your hand safe in mine
> Just lift your cross and
> Follow close to me.

This is so profound! When Christ saves a person, He places an invisible resurrection power in his life. This power goes far beyond his understanding. God makes unlimited energy available, as spoken of here:

> **Therefore, my dear ones, as you have always obeyed (my suggestions), so now, not only (with the enthusiasm you would show) in my presence but much more because I am absent, work out—cultivate, carry out to the goal and fully complete—your own salvation with reverence and awe and trembling (self-distrust, that is, with serious caution, tenderness of conscience, watchfulness against temptation; timidly shrinking from whatever might offend God and discredit the name of Christ). (Not in your own strength), for it is**

God Who is all the while effectually at work in you—energizing and creating in you the power and desire—both to will and to work for His good pleasure and satisfaction and delight (Philippians 2:12-13 Amplified).

There is a ceaseless and growing power in the Christ-pursuing Christian. Christ offers him a level of spiritual dynamics which the believer cannot express or understand until the Holy Spirit reveals it within his spirit. This revelation produces the knowledge of the Power of Jesus' Name and all the fullness of that Name ("all in all"). The will of God is the mind of Christ acting within and through the believer at the level of His conscious understanding. Christ enters into every Christian at the moment of new birth. At this new birth the will of God for his or her life is also placed within. At that moment of salvation the Holy Spirit completely reprograms the Christian and gives him the option of allowing God to live out His will through him. Those who desire to know God must "strive" to know the truth of *"Thy kingdom come, thy will be done..."* They must learn what is happening in heaven and allow God to work it out on earth. The energy of fleshy religious works can never accomplish this.

THEREFORE, [there is] now no condemnation (no adjudging guilty of wrong) for those who are in Christ Jesus, who live [and] walk not after the dictates of the flesh, but after the dictates of the Spirit (Romans 8:1 Amplified).

God does not will just for the Christian to be busy. The Scripture warns us about the danger of becoming *"weary in well doing."* We become dangerously weary when we operate in the power of our flesh and not in the power of the Holy Spirit. *"They that wait upon the Lord shall renew their strength."*

Make Mine a Cadillac

Someone once said jokingly, "I'd be a Baptist, but my

health won't allow it. With all the meetings they have, they're forever going somewhere or doing something." Please understand there is nothing wrong with being busy if it's in the energy of the Spirit and not in the flesh. For when you operate in the power of the Spirit, Christ brings you to a position of revelation according to your level of maturity and growth at that moment.

There are degrees of spiritual maturity, just as there are stages of growth in the human life. When a child is born, it is totally helpless and unable to do anything for itself. However, God provides parental love to secure its future and to maintain its health and care as it begins to grow. (As a personal note, in the case of our household, there is always a Grandma and Grandpa joyfully waiting for an opportunity to share in this wondrous activity.) Foods are specially prepared to fit the dietary needs of the infant. Soon it becomes aware of its surroundings and responds to outside stimulus. The process continues and one day the baby sits up. Then, comes the experience of balancing and standing. Next come baby's first steps with help from those who care. From there, with experience, comes greater balance, strength, and mobility. Then as growth continues the child progresses from single words to understanding sentences. The growing child continues on to paragraphs, then on to a whole language and full oral communication. Finally, there is academic training and a life of its own. These are all part of the process of normal physical growth. I shall allude to this most effective illustration several times in this book. It is the best analogy to God's pattern of spiritual growth.

This is God's way for the new Christian. First comes the inward awareness of who he is: being born again. Then, if he pursues growth through a day-by-day relationship with Christ, there comes the deeper revelation of who he is in Christ. All through the normal Christian experience, there is a constant growing, for no one ever reaches complete maturity. There is always more to *"learn of Me."*

Take My yoke upon you and learn of Me, for I am gentle (meek) and humble (lowly) in

**heart, and you will find rest (relief and ease
and refreshment and recreation and blessed
quiet) for your souls. (Matthew 11:29
Amplified).**

Someone has well said, "As long as you are green, you will
grow; when you get ripe you get rotten." There is no such
thing on earth as a "ripe" Christian. They are all home with
God.

The only way you will experience God's perfect plan for
your life is through constantly seeking Him and His will. As
you do so, He will place within your heart His desires. We
find in Psalms 37:4, *"Delight thyself also in the Lord; and
he shall give thee the desires of thine heart."* Now, this does
not mean He is going to give you a Cadillac when you ask
for it unless it is in His perfect plan. God only promises to
transfer to your heart His personal will and desire according to the level of your growth, understanding, and commitment. This occurs only according to your walk in Him at
the time. Then, upon hearing, you will be able to receive
and act upon His will in faith. This is accomplished only by
"seeking" His mind and will. Another way to say this is, as
you seek Him He will place within your mind the knowledge of His will.

Where Do You Want To Eat?

The word *"delight"* in Psalm 37:4 means we must love
God with a Holy Spirit-enhanced, overwhelming love to be
able to hear from Him. I delight in my wife and will make
any effort to return from a meeting at the earliest possible
convenience. I delight in my children, as well as in their
children, and will make any excuse to go see them. I delight
in my ministry as a vessel allowing the Holy Spirit to
express God's Word through me. I have gone around the
world to do anything that God leads me to do. The word
"delight" means you give yourself totally to God with all joy
and abandon.

The Webster's Dictionary describes the word "delight":
"to rejoice, especially with feelings or display of triumph or
self-satisfaction." In this case, there is a willingness to do

anything He desires because of your overwhelming love for Him and your complete joy in serving Him. In fact, you delight in surrendering all to His control. When that happens, then the Holy Spirit, by the *"hope of glory,"* speaks to your mind intuitively at the level of your maturity. Again, the hearing comes to babies in Christ differently than it does to those who are growing in grace and knowledge, but it does come.

The verse continues, *"He will give you the desires of your heart."* In your *"delight"* you abandon yourself totally to Him. Your inward desire then becomes fully open to His will for your life. God has already programmed you with His design for your life.

> **For we are God's [own] handiwork (His workmanship), recreated in Christ Jesus, [born anew] that we may do those good works which God predestined (planned beforehand) for us [taking paths which He prepared ahead of time], that we should walk in them [living the good life which He prearranged and made ready for us to live] (Ephesians 2:10 Amplified).**

Your delight in Him engages the switch of His will. I know this to be so. You will do everything in your power to please one whom you truly love. As you do He will reveal His will through you.

My wife and I have had the same conversation over and over during our forty two years of marriage. I say to her,

"Where do you want to eat?"

She will always respond, "I don't care. Where do you want to eat?"

We go through this constantly. I want to please her; she will respond in the same way. Well, perhaps not always the same. She does have a change of attitude when I mention Chinese food. The true test of our relationship comes many times when she will go and say nothing. However, she displays her attitude in the way she clicks her chopsticks. She still goes with me, and that is love: though I do on occasion have to dodge the splinters.

In the same kind of love, when we long for the Bridegroom, we will keep our lamps trimmed and ready in expectation of His Coming. Our delight in Him always brings His desire or will to our lives. We know it and operate in it. As we grow we will structure our lives to please Him. (I will speak more of Psalm 37:4 later in this writing.)

What's In it For Me?

This is also the message of Romans 12:1-2—constantly yielding your life to Christ. As you do you will respond to His working from the inside out. To say it in a better way, you allow Christ who lives within to begin to live through you without.

> **I beseech you therefore, brethren, by the mercies of God, that ye present your bodies a living sacrifice, holy, acceptable unto God, which is your reasonable service. And be not conformed to this world: but be ye transformed by the renewing of your mind, that ye may prove what is that good, and acceptable, and perfect, will of God (Romans 12:1-2).**

Now, let's begin to study the principles of finding God's personal will for your life. Paul opens Romans 12:1 with, *"I beseech you."* In these closing chapters of Romans, the Holy Spirit determines to bring home the truth of the transformed life. He begs for the attention of his readers so they will adhere to these truths. In chapters 6 through 8 of this epistle, He constantly alludes to the fact that nothing in dead religion works. He constantly admonishes his hearers with the fact that only Christ Himself living His life through them will work.

To get their attention, he begins the verse by using the word *"beseech,"* which means "to implore or to beg." He must bring them to focus their attention on this vital truth. Without its meaning revealed in them all their Christian life will be the activity of the "flesh."

He continues with the word *"therefore."* The Scripture uses this term to indicate the subject of the prior verse(s) is still being addressed. From chapter eleven Paul continues to proclaim the reality that everything belongs to God. The same is true in the life of every Christian. When the Holy Spirit draws us through conviction and repentance of sin to seek salvation by grace through faith, we are at that moment born from above. God then becomes our Heavenly Father. Therefore, when we give ourselves over to who we are in Him, we then come to what we truly were meant to be. We become one with Christ and alive in Him.

For this reason, Paul declares to the readers of this letter, *"I beseech you, therefore, brethren, by the mercies of God..."* To bring his point to the Roman Christians into clearer focus, he uses the word *"mercies."* The thought here is, because of Christ's life, death, resurrection, and all He paid, they should yield everything to Him. Again, we must understand that God's will can be established and performed through us only when we constantly pursue Christ and abandon our lives to Him.

Paul continues to develop this truth in these verses. He had already established in Romans that, because of God's willingness to give up His Son, and Christ's willingness to come to earth and die for us, we should be ready to yield our lives totally to Christ's will. Only when we get home to Heaven, and we are in our glorified minds, will we truly understand the reason. We will see the reality of what Jesus has done in our behalf and it will overwhelm us there. Because of it we will worship before the throne of God forever. However, God also wants us to recognize it here, and then by choice to live it! Paul is begging the Roman Christians to see it. We will constantly refer to Romans 12:1-2 throughout this book. It will be the thread that holds together the fabric of the truth of finding God's will.

The usual procedure that God uses to bring an individual into true ministry is to first reveal Himself to him. In that encounter, he sees himself as God sees him and is shattered over his unrighteousness. Finally, he enters into a ministry that is no longer his, but God's. We must understand that no one will ever be mightily used of God until all of self is unveiled and is purged by an inward desire to be broken.

— Mickey Bonner

Chapter Two

God, Show Me—Me

I have experienced the wonders of answered prayer many times. Many are vivid in my memory. Two, however, had such profound impact they are imprinted indelibly on my life. The first was in March 1953 when I confessed my sins and believed in the Lord Jesus Christ to save me, and He did. I was truly born again and transformed into a new creature in Christ.

The second occurred in 1971 in Chateau d'Oex, Switzerland at a Bible Conference. I became deeply convinced that God did not have all of me. One evening after a glorious service, I was under deep personal conviction. I walked the halls of the hotel all night in agony of soul. My constant prayer to God was, "What is wrong in my life? What are you saying to me?" Finally, at dawn, in a state of deep, overwhelming contrition, I cried out for help. I begged Him in prayer to tell me what He wanted me to say to Him. Intuitively I heard, "Lord, reveal me to me as You see me." I remember blurting that cry out loud. He, in quick response, opened for me the door to my true life and self. I broke under the revelation. I saw for the first time what I truly was.

What God showed me was definitely not what I had tried to make others believe about me. Oh, the perversion, the filth, and most of all the pride! I understood fully Paul's declaration, *"O, wretched man that I am."* In today's vernacular, "It wiped me out." I was devastated and totally embarrassed.

Something life-changing happened to me early that morning. From that moment I have continued to beg God to get me out of the business and game of worldly Christian activity. I have desired from that moment to experience the life of Christ. In fact, on that day, I made a deal with God that I would cease trying to be a Christian according to what I had been taught. Furthermore, I would begin to seek daily the sovereign will of God in my life.

Beloved, thousands of times, through satan's wiles, I have fallen away from that growing place. However, as my rebellion brought separation and chastisement from the Lord, from the depths of loneliness and longing in my heart, I always have fought to re-establish a right relationship with Him. I want to praise and thank Him for He continually brings me to brokenness by chastening. He will not let me go for He knows, in spite of myself, I truly desire restitution and restoration with Him. Oh, the overwhelming joy of walking in the Spirit, and the inner longing to stay within that realm of living victory!

> **But the fruit of the [Holy] Spirit [the work which His presence within accomplishes] is love, joy (gladness), peace, patience (an even temper, forbearance), kindness, goodness (benevolence), faithfulness. Gentleness (meekness, humility), self-control (self-restraint, continence). Against such things there is no law [that can bring a charge]. And those who belong to Christ Jesus (the Messiah) have crucified the flesh (the godless human nature) with its passions and appetites and desires (Galatians 5:22-24 Amplified).**

However, I do on occasion begin to slide back in response to the circumstances satan produces to cause my flesh to come alive. Then the conditions described in Galatians 5:19-21 dominate me again:

Now the doings (practices) of the flesh are clearly obvious: they are immorality, impurity, indecency; Idolatry, sorcery, enmity, strife, jealousy, anger (ill temper), selfishness, divisions (dissensions), party spirit (factions, sects with peculiar opinions, heresies); Envy, drunkenness, carousing, and the like. I warn you beforehand, just as I did previously, that those who do such things shall not inherit the kingdom of God (Amplified).

Because of this overwhelming demonic pull of the flesh the believer must choose to stay on the offense and attack it with the sword of praise.

Let the high praises of God be in their mouth, and the two-edged sword in their hand (Psalm 149:6).

By the power of the sword of the Spirit he or she can overcome satan's every temptation. This spiritual warfare praying will keep the believer from losing his abundant life in Christ. If he does not take this stand he will distance himself from the voice of God and will not hear or understand His will. In the process, the believer will give place to the devil. By his own act of carnality, he will lose the knowledge of God's will and direction in his life. If he repents, this loss will be only temporary. If he persists, this unguarded way becomes a place of darkness and loneliness as he falls into the pit satan has "digged for his soul."

For without cause have they hid for me their net [in] a pit, [which] without cause they have digged for my soul (Psalms 35:7).

How often in my Christian journey have I awakened to realize I have lost that precious relationship with the Lord

Jesus Christ and had to begin again the battle to return!

If this has happened to you, I urge you, at this moment, to begin to pursue the Lord Jesus and drink deeply of His life. Force yourself toward Him. Desire to be His more than you want anything else in the world. You must act personally. If you don't, you will not grow in Christ. Regarding this, the Scripture states:

> **In the last day, that great day of the feast, Jesus stood and cried, saying, If any man thirst, let him come unto me, and drink. He that believeth on me, as the scripture hath said, out of his belly shall flow rivers of living water (John 7:37-38).**

God has made a great declaration concerning our place in righteousness. Probably the best translation of this verse is in the Weymouth rendition of the Greek in these verses. He translates two phrases in John 7:37-38 particularly well. They describe God's desire for the growing Christian. In verse 37 we read, *"Drink deeply of the Spirit of God."* Then, in verse 38 he states, *"He that believeth into me..."* This is, in essence, the divine truth of finding His will. *"Drink deeply"* and then *"believe into."* What a revelation! We must seek after Christ by our complete surrender to Him.

Seven Times a Day

To begin to build on God's will you must share with Him constantly that you love Him and act accordingly. Then have times of praise with Him at least seven times a day, for the Scripture teaches: *"Seven times a day do I praise thee because of thy righteous judgments"* (Psalm 119:164). From that point of pursuing or actively chasing His presence, you will then come to joy, victory, and great peace. This idea of pursuing God is beautifully seen in I Peter 3:11-12. The Greek word for pursue, *"dioko,"* means "seeking eagerly." Experiencing Christ's life will cause you to drive your life constantly to His personal will. In that relationship you will know not only *"joy unspeakable"* and "peace that passeth all understanding," but you will then begin to live the life of the person of Christ as well. His life through you will bring the abundant life into your heart. From this place only will you begin to glimpse the total will of God for your life.

A Desire to Please Dad

As a child, I never experienced a close father/son relationship. My dad worked night and day coming out of the Great Depression in the 1930s. His driving desire was to succeed as a small, independent businessman. In the financial world, he did. At home, however, I never knew him because of his work schedule. His actions toward me were no more than reaction to the negative aspects of my life; I could do nothing right. How true the Scriptures that teach:

> **Fathers, do not irritate and provoke your children to anger—do not exasperate them to resentment—but rear them (tenderly) in the training and discipline and the counsel and admonition of the Lord (Ephesians 6:4, Amplified).**

> **Fathers do not provoke or irritate or fret your children—do not be hard on them or harass them; lest they become discouraged and sullen and morose and feel inferior and frustrated; do not break their spirit (Col. 3:21, Amplified).**

I have written in my book *What's Wrong With America: Satan's Attack on the Home*, "A father will treat his children the way he was treated." I knew no love from my father. Through this, satan saw to it that I blamed my dad for all of my conflicts and failures. My childhood and young adulthood lacked any depth or direction. Consequently, I was unable to express love to my own children in the early years of their lives.

After my salvation experience at age 23 and after serving on the staff of two churches, I spent eighteen months as a pastor. From there, I entered into full-time evangelism. I spent most of those years of ministry as an emotional cripple. Not until age 38 did the proper healing in this area begin. I had to forgive and get right with my dad before any kind of true spiritual growth could begin in me.

When I made restitution to my father (a spiritual imperative), God began to open the door of hearing from Him. With it came the realization that I was doing to my children what my dad had done to me. God's revelation had begun. I nearly destroyed the lives of my own children. I disciplined them as I had been disciplined: always in anger. I broke their spirits. How tragic!

The proper way to express my condition is my personal paraphrase of a verse of Scripture to read: "What does it profit a man to gain a ministry and lose his own family?" When God, through His chastisement in my life, revealed my wrong feelings, He made me make them right through forgiveness. Through this breaking within, I fell in love with my dad. He turned out to be an incredible individual, especially when I saw him through the eyes of the Holy Spirit. I found that I wanted to please him for the first time in my life. As always happens when repentance comes, God performed a miracle in my life. From that moment on, things began to come together in my ministry and, especially, in my home. I have written two books on this that deal with this subject fully: *God Can Heal Your Mind*, and *What's Wrong With America—Satan's Attack on the Home*. These contain the details of the transition of my life back to God's will. Thank God for His Wonderful Mercy and Grace!

Love is the Key

What is the point of all of this? Though we lived together in our home, I had no communication with my family. I would hear what they said, but I was too busy to want to understand. Communication was one-way—my way or no way. I usually administered my way by angry force. I heard their voices, but because of my selfish, bitter, carnal life, I chose not to listen or comprehend. How true this is of the average Christian and his relationship to his heavenly Father. He has a one-way conversation toward God. He is a carnal and self-willed baby so he cannot comprehend what he hears. He talks *to* God, but he will not hear *from* God. He does not understand that love is the key to hearing and the bridge to all communication.

Since this work of grace happened to me in Switzerland, I find I must walk with God. This compulsion comes now from desperate desire. Again, as stated in the first chapter, I liken this to a child's stages of growth. During the first months of a baby's life he is wrapped up in appeasing his own personality. When he has a need, he cries. Someone responds in love, and takes care of it.

As the baby grows, he comes to a day of reckoning as his parents establish the principles and positions of obedience in his life. They do this to bring the baby within the confines of the standards of life and authority. With it comes the "yes" and "no" teachings of what to touch or not to touch—what to do or not to do. In fact, the child's first word of true comprehension (for the most part) is "no."

Hair on His Chest

Children born since Adam are brought into this world conceived in sin. Their very nature will develop to the sin side of their lives. In the home, there must be loving reprimands. Parents do this in order for the child to discover the directions and conditions that are the rule in the household. This continues all through the young life to achieve a proper inner balance to human existence. God states in His Word, *"Train up a child in the way he should go, and when he is old, he will not depart from it"* (Proverbs 22:6). It is the same in the kingdom of God. He has a purpose and plan for every Christian's life. We find this all through God's Word, but especially in Hebrews 12:5-12:

> **"And ye have forgotten the exhortation which speaketh unto you as unto children, My son, despise not thou the chastening of the Lord, nor faint when thou art rebuked of him: For whom the Lord loveth he chasteneth, and scourgeth every son whom he receiveth. If ye endure chastening, God dealeth with you as with sons; for what son is he whom the father chasteneth not? But if ye be without chastisement, whereof all are partakers, then are ye**

bastards, and not sons. Furthermore we have had fathers of our flesh which corrected us, and we gave them reverence: shall we not much rather be in subjection unto the Father of spirits, and live? For they verily for a few days chastened us after their own pleasure; but he for our profit, that we might be partakers of his holiness. Now no chastening for the present seemeth to be joyous, but grievous; nevertheless afterward it yieldeth the peaceable fruit of righteousness unto them which are exercised thereby. Wherefore lift up the hands which hang down, and the feeble knees."

In these passages, God speaks of chastising in the believer's life. A term better understood in this day is discipline. He does this to conform us to His image and bring us into His will. He does it for our own good and His glory. It is noteworthy that the word for "chastening" in verse 5 is the Greek word *"paideia."* Its meaning has to do with child training. This, again, parallels Ephesians 6:4. Here God commands the father: *"Provoke not your children to wrath."* Parents who discipline in anger will set the course for the child's entire life. It reacts to others in anger for the rest of its life unless the Lord brings healing. This reaction demonstrates the position of the Scripture: *"Train up a child in the way he should go; and when he is old he will not depart from it"* (Proverbs 22:6). I read somewhere years ago that the Jews gauged the "old" spoken of here as the time when hair appears on the chest of a young man.

Again, provoking a child to anger prepares a fertile soil for all demonic forces to plant corruption or disruption in the individual for a lifetime. God commands the father to correct in love, not to punish (discipline) in anger. This kind of punishment finds its roots in revenge. The dad acts out his hostilities on those who cannot react on their own. However, the tragedy is that satan places these events deep in their minds and they never forget. From there, "the roots of bitterness" wait for a time and place to act out their own rage on a helpless victim.

Seeing is Doing

Beloved, here is help for a lifetime. My hostilities to my children were a reaction to my experience with my own father. Therefore, my hearing from God was hindered. I know that now. Through my reactions, I broke their spirit, destroying, through a root of bitterness, their walk with God in revelation. Looking at the rest of Ephesians 6:4, we find God commands the father to bring up his children *"in the nurture and admonition of the Lord."* God commands the father to lead his babies in Spiritual things. They will observe his spiritual nature as he demonstrates it through his life. Through his daily witness, they will begin yielding to God in their early age by learning his attributes. Here they will see and experience answered prayer through the life of the dad. Because of this, they will never in their lifetime be alone. Nor will they grow up without having witnessed God's glory in their parents' lives. As the old adage says, "Seeing is doing."

Such is the thought in Hebrews 12, with the word *"paideia"* (chastening). In a similar way, God continues discipline and child training in the believer's life. This is the reason for chastening (discipline). God corrects us to keep us living within the confines of family life in the household of faith. He does this also so we will begin to mature into the will of God. We are to look like, act like, and be like our Father. In the process of this, we experience growth which brings understanding.

> **Lean on, trust in, and be confident in the Lord with all your heart and mind and do not rely on your own insight or understanding (Proverbs 3:5 Amplified).**

You say, "What does all of this have to do with finding God's will?" God's discipline is the first step to hearing.

Purifying the Vessel

(This section was taken from my book, *Brokenness, the Forgotten Factor of Prayer*, and edited for use here.)

No one will ever truly see Christ for who He really is, except through brokenness and tears. For brokenness to come, one's heart must be truly repentant, thereby crucifying the old man within him. Purging through real repentance and the revelation of personal sins must occur. Anger must be nailed to the cross. Lust, guilt, pride, and the rest of the flesh's control, must be put in its place. Complete abandonment to God must take precedence in the life of that individual. When a person is completely broken over what he is, and ardent repentance overwhelms his sin, the light of God's Spirit begins to shine inward to reveal the reality of His righteousness and the purity of His person. In that state, the believer is completely broken before God and ready for His will and ministry to be performed through his life. He must seek after it. Isaiah's experience in the sixth chapter of his book demonstrates this process.

In the year that king Uzziah died I saw also the Lord sitting upon a throne, high and lifted up, and his train filled the temple. Above it stood the seraphims: each one had six wings; with twain he covered his face, and with twain he covered his feet, and with twain he did fly. And one cried unto another, and said, Holy, holy, holy, is the Lord of hosts: the whole earth is full of his glory. And the posts of the door moved at the voice of him that cried, and the house was filled with smoke. Then said I, Woe is me! for I am undone; because I am a man of unclean lips, and I dwell in the midst of a people of unclean lips: for mine eyes have seen the King, the Lord of hosts. Then flew one of the seraphims unto me, having a live coal in his hand, which he had taken from off the altar: And he laid it upon my mouth, and said, Lo, this hath touch thy lips; and thine iniquity is taken away, and thy sin purged. Also I heard the voice of the Lord, saying, Whom shall I send, and who will go for us? Then said I, Here am I; send me (Isaiah 6:1-8).

After much study, I personally believe that Isaiah's experience was one of brokenness. It prepared him as a messenger for the great prophecies of the revelation of God concerning the birth of His Son as He came through the womb of a virgin woman. He would come to this world in the flesh as God incarnate, and would live a sinless life, that He might become sin for us. He would be led as a sheep to the slaughter, silent before his accusers, to be nailed to a cross. He would then die a death so far beyond any human experience that even *"His visage was marred more than any man."*

Physically, every bone would be poured out like water, meaning all would be out of joint. His blood would flow from His body as He would hang upon the cross. In the meantime, this event in history would cause even the sun to be blotted out and the earth to shake. Jesus would then be laid in the grave. Peace would falsely abound and the world's religious system would be brought to a calm again. Suddenly, that grave would open and a three-day-dead body would come forth, risen alive from the grave!

It was in actuality, the beginning of a true new-world order in a new day that would have its birth on the morning of Pentecost, when the Holy Spirit would come. Such was the preparation of this announcement and its declaration. The pure truth of the matter in these verses of Chapter 6 is that the man Isaiah is being made ready to share the greatest event of all human history: the coming Messiah, known as *"Wonderful, Counselor, The mighty God, The everlasting Father, The Prince of peace," (Isaiah 9:6)*—Jesus.

What was about to happen in Isaiah's life was not just to get his attention, but to pierce to the deepest core of his innermost being, thereby bringing into union with his spirit the presence of the Holy Spirit of God. So it was when Isaiah raised his eyes in the presence of God, and saw the Lord sitting on the throne, (Isaiah 6:1-2). *"high and lifted up and his train filled the temple."* Then he saw above it the seraphim. *"each one had six wings; with twain he covered his face, and with twain, he covered his feet and with twain he did fly."*

Isaiah is being readied by God to receive the message of His coming Son and to have it burned deep into his heart.

We find basically woven through every verse of this book, from that moment on, the wonderful presence of the person of Jesus Christ, as well as the holiness of God.

In the light of this, you will find that the usual procedure that God uses to bring an individual into true ministry is to first reveal Himself to him. In that encounter, he sees himself as God sees him and is shattered over his unrighteousness. Finally, he enters into a ministry that is no longer his, but God's. This is God's biblical pattern, and over the years I have personally experienced it in my own life. Also, I have observed others through whom He extended His will.

With this pattern in mind, let's see how God dealt with the prophet Isaiah. First of all, Isaiah saw himself after seeing God. By scriptural example, God revealed everything about Himself to Isaiah: His throne, His heaven, and His presence as light. It forever changed the course of Isaiah's life and ministry; for it began the disintegration of pride and flesh and birthed a man totally committed to God.

Remember, when Isaiah saw God, he saw himself. This always happens for someone to be fully used of God. Now, look back at his procedure of repentance. The first thing he said was, *"Woe is me. I am undone."* For the first time, he saw himself as only God could see him. The level of unrighteousness was so overwhelming that he cried in agony before the Lord. He could not believe his own observation. We must understand that no one will ever be mightily used of God until all of self is unveiled and is purged by an inward desire to be broken.

At the moment God revealed Himself, Isaiah broke before His presence. Again, when a man truly sees in himself what God sees, he will be exposed to what he really is in the eyes of God, even though he may feel he has done his best for God. He will, at that point, be shattered.

To understand what God was doing in the preparation of Isaiah for the revelation of Christ's life, let's review again what happens when a person is broken over who he is. First, he sees himself as God sees him. In that encounter, he is devastated over the sin in his own life. No matter how righteous he appears to be to others, or even to himself, something profoundly happens to the person. In God's presence Isaiah realized he was unclean. He was undone when he saw himself through God. Isaiah then tells the why of his depravity; *"Because I am a man of unclean lips."* God teaches in His Word that it is not what goes into a person's mouth that defiles him; it is what comes out.

> **Not that which goeth into the mouth defileth a man; but that which cometh out of the mouth, this defileth a man (Matthew 15:11).**

Your confession broadcasts your real character and sets the course of your life, (James 3:6).

Now, in continued preparation of Isaiah for God's ministry, there was yet a work to be done to his lips. God, in order to use this man, was to do a final purging of his confession. The Lord then sent one of the seraphim to Isaiah, *"having a live coal in his hand which he had taken with the tongs from off the altar."* He laid it upon the lips of Isaiah that God might purge from the prophet all indication of self, desire, negative confession, and critical words. He literally burned (cauterized) his lips to such a degree that not only were they spiritually seared, destroying all negativity, but they were sealed for a lifetime of service as an oracle of God.

In review of the events leading to his brokenness, we find that Isaiah saw the Lord. He then saw himself and was devastated and cried in true repentance for forgiveness. In progression, God then purged his confession and changed the course, or direction, of what proceeded out of Isaiah's mouth. When we see God and are broken, and our confession is cleansed, suddenly our ears are clear to hear the voice of God's will. Spiritual ears were placed within Isaiah during the process of his breaking. From the presence of the temple, God suddenly cried out, *"Whom shall I send, and who will go for us?"* Isaiah heard the cry and responded. It is amazing how tribulation will tune the believer's hearing to God's frequency.

Signs of Salvation

I am my father's son. People used to stop my dad on the

street and ask if he were Arthur Godfrey, an entertainer well-known in that day. For years, people have said that I look like this same television personality. However, as I grow in Christ through discipline and God's constant plan for my development, my deepest desire is to look more like my heavenly Father every day. To do so, God must inevitably bring chastisement, correction, and discipline in my life. Their purpose is to change me into my Father's likeness and keep me in His will.

Also, my being chastised or dealt with by God in correction, is living proof that I have been born again. This demonstrates the vital truth that I am His son by adoption. I am a part of the family of God and He will not allow His born again children to remain in sin. A loving father will always oversee his children's development and take an active part in their lifestyles. God, our Father, does the same.

To firmly place this in our minds, let us look once more at God's sequence of discipline. To begin, when disobedience enters the life of the believer, God begins the work of restoring that person to His will. As we stated earlier, His first mode of correction is chastisement or the dealing with the circumstance in His child's life. He begins by causing conflicts in circumstances, relationships, associations, or even finances, to get the Christian's attention and bring him back into His will.

> **Consider it wholly joyful, my brethren, whenever you are enveloped in or encounter trials of any sort or fall into various temptations. Be assured and understand that the trial and proving of your faith bring out endurance and steadfastness and patience (James 1:2-3 Amplified).**

If this does not work and the believer rebels or "bows his neck" against the Father's authority, He then moves into scourging. Hebrews 12:6 tells us the Father disciplines us and scourges every son whom He receives. Now, the Greek word here for scourging is *"mastigoo,"* which means "to whip, flog, or beat." If the Christian continues in rebellion against God's will, then He allows satan to move upon the flesh of the rebel. A dear friend of mine, Dr. J. Harold

Smith, preaches a message called *God's Three Deadlines.* He declares the final move of God upon His rebellious child who will not return to His will after chastening and scourging, is death. Proverbs 29:1 clearly states that *"he that is often reproved and hardeneth his neck shall suddenly be destroyed and that without remedy."* God allows the flesh to be destroyed that the individual might be saved *"passed through fire"*

If any man's work shall be burned, he shall suffer loss: but he himself shall be saved; yet so as by fire (I Corinthians 3:15).

By contrast, when the believer submits to God's correction (chastening) as an obedient, non-rebellious child, he will begin to develop his hearing from the Holy Spirit. These disciplinary processes will bring, in every occasion, a measure of spiritual growth. The believer experiences this in his daily walk.

For this reason, because I have heard of your faith in the Lord Jesus and your love toward all the saints (the people of God), I do not cease to give thanks for you, making mention of you in my prayers. [For I always pray to] the God of our Lord Jesus Christ, the Father of glory, that He may grant you a spirit of wisdom and revelation [of insight into mysteries and secrets] in the [deep and intimate] knowledge of Him. By having the eyes of your heart flooded with light, so that you can know and understand the hope to which He has called you, and how rich is His glorious inheritance in the saints (His set-apart ones), And [so that you can know and understand] what is the immeasurable and unlimited and surpassing greatness of His power in and for us who believe, as demonstrated in the working of His mighty strength, Which He exerted in Christ when He raised Him from the dead and seated Him at his [own] right hand in the

heavenly [places], Far above all rule and authority and power and dominion and every name that is named [above every title that can be conferred], not only in this age and in this world, but also in the age and the world which are to come. And He has put all things under His feet and has appointed Him the universal and supreme Head of the church [a headship exercised throughout the church], Which is His body, the fullness of Him Who fills all in all [for in that body lives the full measure of Him Who makes everything complete, and Who fills everything everywhere with Himself]. (Ephesians 1:15-23 Amplified).

From there, the hearing quality of his prayer life improves. All the events of breaking are God's education process in our spiritual growth and life. How wonderful! The chastening of God is, again, for our good and His glory. Remember, all chastening is for our profit that we might be partakers of His holiness or be one with Him in the Spirit.*"They disciplined us for a short time as seemed right to them, but he does so for our benefit, in order that we may share his holiness"* (Hebrews 12:10 emphasis added).

Peaceable Fruit

Our Father's discipline is the primary factor in our growth, and path to our finding the mind of God. All processes of growth are based on discipline, whether it is by self-correction and study, or by authoritative instruction from the Father. It is all for our maturity.

As I look back on my journey with God, verse 11 has become so real to me: *"Now no chastening for the present seemeth to be joyous, but grievous: nevertheless afterward it yieldeth the peaceable fruit of righteousness unto them which are exercised thereby."* As God began preparing me for His work at the level of my obedience, I would complain about what I was going through. My own self-pity and all I could gather from others through complaining were ever present in my prolonged, self-centered, baby state. However, as I look back to the conflicts and recognize the hand of God, I see He used those times to make Himself more real and sufficient to me in every way. How marvelously true is the verse that says: *"Thou hast enlarged me when I was in distress"* (Psalms 4:1).

Thus, by the school of discipline, God brings His students into new levels of His kingdom's work. They become knowledgeable graduates whom He has broken into practicing the "living Word" as the life of Christ consumes them. They have learned to hear, understand, and then obey. Beloved, God says in I Samuel 15:26: *"to obey is better than sacrifice."* In God's way (Spirit), obedience transcends sacrifice. Man's way (flesh) is mere religion, and sacrifice in the form of religious observance is paramount. As His students grow by obedience, the Holy Spirit does increasingly profound work through them by the Holy Spirit (Luke 12:48).

I cannot emphasize strongly enough that this is the test of knowing if you have been born again. It is not the way you deal with God in religious activity, but how He deals with you in correction and discipline as your heavenly Father.

Now, let me change directions here for the moment in order for you to apply what we are saying to your personal life. The Scripture teaches that you are to *"examine yourselves whether ye be in the faith."*

Examine and test and evaluate your own selves to see whether you are holding to your faith and showing the proper fruits of it. Test and prove yourselves [not Christ]. Do you not yourselves realize and know [thoroughly by an ever-increasing experience] that Jesus Christ is in you—unless you are [counterfeits] disapproved on trial and rejected? (II Corinthians 13:5 Amplified)

Untold millions, who in their lifetime thought they possessed salvation, will stand before God someday at the judgment of the lost.

And I saw a great white throne, and him that sat on it, from whose face the earth and

the heaven fled away; and there was found no place for them (Revelation 20:11).

They will cry before Him that they "believed" in their lifetime. Many of those will have experienced spirit-manifestations of the power to perform demon deliverances and healings all in the Name of Jesus. The tragedy of it all is that these works were done in the name of the wrong Jesus.

For if he that cometh preacheth another Jesus, whom we have not preached, or if ye receive another spirit, which ye have not received, or another gospel, which ye have not accepted, ye might well bear with him. For I suppose I was not a whit behind the very chiefest apostles (II Corinthians 11:4-5).

They will declare themselves not only to have known Christ, but to have operated in the Holy Spirit's power. How tragic it will be when they hear, one-by-one, that their names were never recorded in the Lamb's Book of Life and they are commanded to depart! No wailing ever experienced in history will be like their cries of despair! To be taken by God and cast into the lake of fire, oh, the horrible tragedy of an eternity without Christ! As a religious person, do you know for sure that you have been born again? It is imperative. Without new birth, you will never know the mind of Christ. You must first of all have Him living within. As the old gospel hymn says, you must "Turn Your Radio On." To make the unit work you must first have power (salvation and the Holy Spirit living within). Then you must have the knowledge (obedience) to tune to the station to receive the signal.

[For I always pray to] the God of our Lord Jesus Christ, the Father of glory, that He may grant you a spirit of wisdom and revelation [of insight into mysteries and secrets] in the [deep and intimate] knowledge of Him (Ephesians 1:17 Amplified).

All of our experiences can be processes of growth if we learn "to hear" the Savior. The voice of Jesus comes to you only on His own frequency; and you must understand His language when hearing.

Charles Finney's new birth experience and his filling of the Holy Spirit are described in his own words in the Appendix. This story demonstrates how a life can be totally transformed and tuned into the will of God as the Spirit of God makes its home in a man.

Finding God's will means going after Christ with all of your heart, soul, and mind. It means pursuing Jesus Christ every moment in every matter until you are conditioned to His voice either through reading the Word or the Holy Spirit guiding from the inside to direct your steps. This is the biblical condition the Holy Spirit lays out for the committed child of God to receive direction from Him. As you constantly *yield* your life, you will begin to *receive* the personal will of God.

— Mickey Bonner

Chapter Three

Time for the Test

Before moving on to the study of the place of spiritual hearing in Christianity, let us examine once more the reasons believers cannot hear the voice of God within their spirits. The Bible teaches that the Holy Spirit lives in the born-again child of God.

> **And grieve not the Holy Spirit of God, whereby ye are sealed unto the day of redemption (Ephesians 4:30).**

He also has a personal daily plan for that individual. The saved who are growing will be led of the Spirit. Those who are not growing and refuse to be led will stumble and operate in darkness. Their experience of the Christian life, as stated earlier, will be the life of the flesh described in Galatians 5:19-22.

> **The works of the flesh are manifest, which are [these]; adultery, fornication, uncleanness, lasciviousness, idolatry, witchcraft, hatred,**

variance, emulations, wrath, strife, seditions, heresies, Envyings, murders, drunkenness, revellings, and such like: of the which I tell you before, as I have also told [you] in time past, that they which do such things shall not inherit the kingdom of God. But the fruit of the Spirit is love, joy, peace, longsuffering, gentleness, goodness, faith (Galatians 5:19-22).

Therefore, to better understand our place in Him, let us pause here to take a Scriptural test of your personal position in Christ. To begin, you must again Scripturally check your new birth by God's biblical plan of salvation. That means testing your born again experience against Bible truths.

First of all, do you truly believe in God? Do you believe the biblical account of His life and existence in eternity past, present, and future? Do you believe He has a Son named Jesus Christ who chose to leave heaven and come to this earth to be born of a virgin? Do you believe He lived His life without sin? Do you believe He then gave His life on a cross, and while doing so, He bore all the sins of humanity, from the beginning of history to its end? Do you believe that He, by His choice, bore your own personal sins on Calvary?

In essence, this means He knew you personally by name. He knew the thoughts and intents and doings of your life. Do you believe then that your sins, as well as all of the sins in the history of man, single and composite, were laid upon Him and paid for by His blood? Do you believe He, by His own choice, then yielded up His Spirit and died, only to rise again alive and triumphant in three days? Do you also believe that after His being raised from the dead He was visibly seen by hundreds? Then, on an appointed day, He rose to take His place by the right hand of God? Can you accept that He will return at the end of the age to bring with Him those saved who have gone on before, and take those alive in Christ home with Him? Do you believe all of that? Well, so do the devil and his angels, and they tremble.

> **You believe that God is one; you do well. So
> do the demons believe and shudder [in terror
> and horror such as make a man's hair stand
> on end and contract the surface of his skin]!
> (James 2:19 Amplified)**

Believing is not enough for eternal salvation. There is another step.

"Gutter-Most"

The Scriptures are adamant about true salvation. God says: *"For all have sinned and come short of the glory of God"* (Romans 3:23). In this verse, we find that all are sinners; therefore, all must have a Savior. Then, the second step to salvation is to understand you have sinned: *"For the wages of sin is death; but the gift of God is eternal life through Jesus Christ our Lord"* (Romans 6:23).

Although the book of Romans was written for Christians, we find in its text the pattern for salvation. Here God says that if we die in our sins we will face (for eternity) separation in Hell. However, included in that verse is the statement that there is a gift extended to those who will receive Him. That gift is eternal life.

Incidentally, a gift is something that cannot be earned. It must be received for free and not for labor. The great tragedy of eternity will be the millions of lost church members who cry out to God at the judgment that they were born again. They feel they have achieved new birth through their baptism, catechism, confirmation, or work and service by physical activity. The terrible truth of this is that they are lost—forever!

> **And besides all this, between us and you a
> great chasm has been fixed, in order that
> those who want to pass from this [place] to
> you may not be able, and no one may pass
> from there to us (Luke 16:26 Amplified).**

Then, the third step, you must receive Him: *"But as*

many as received him, to them gave he power to become the sons of God, even to them that believe on his name" (John 1:12). To be saved, you must open your life by believing in Him in faith. You must want Him with all your heart. Finally, we are told by John that He is standing at the door of every person's life, wanting to come in. He desires to save. He has made the way of redemption through His blood. He will save anyone who will repent: from the "guttermost" to the "uttermost"! You must make sure of this calling in your heart.

Behold, I stand at the door, and knock: if any man hear my voice, and open the door, I will come in to him, and will sup with him, and he with me (Revelation 3:20).

By establishing your new birth, you will set in motion your ability to hear from God regarding His will. Just to make your salvation sure, let me urge you right now to pray this prayer from the depth of all you are—meaning every word:

"Father, in the name of Jesus, I believe in You with all of my heart; I believe You sent Christ for me. I believe He died for my sins. I am a sinner, oh, God; I have sinned. I come to You now in Jesus Christ's name confessing all that I have done. Forgive me of all of my sins. Thank You for your forgiveness. Lord Jesus Christ, come into my heart and save me. Thank You for saving my soul. And now fill me with Your Spirit. I claim my salvation and filling in Jesus Christ's name."

Salvation Settled

If you were lost and truly convicted and broken over your sin, and desired God's forgiveness and salvation, you were just born again. Also, you knew it when it happened. Oh, my beloved, are you truly saved? You must be in order to hear and find God's personal will for your life. This first step is imperative. With this experience, the Holy Spirit comes to dwell within you. From that place alone will He guide you into all truth.

> **But when He, the Spirit of Truth (the Truth-giving Spirit) comes, He will guide you into all the Truth (the whole, full Truth). For He will not speak His own message [on His own authority]; but He will tell whatever He hears [from the Father; He will give the message that has been given to Him], and He will announce and declare to you the things that are to come [that will happen in the future] (John 16:13 Amplified).**

Your place is to seek and to stay in His will. To remain in that place of hearing, you must constantly present your body as a living sacrifice to God. To hear from Him within, or to hear Him through the Scriptures, you must give up everything you are to Him. You must lay down who you are and what you can do for Him. You must cast aside your own abilities and "present"—and keep on presenting—your total person to Christ. You must develop an overwhelming desire within to do whatever it takes to make you totally abandon self. In this case, your prayer should be:

> *"Father, in the name of Jesus, put me within that realm of Your will and tear away these man-patterned Christian experiences in my life. Tear down the rebellion. Take it away that I might be filled with the person of Christ and that I might actively live in His personal will and operate in His personal plan for my life. Whatever it takes to break me, do it. Oh, God, do it, and thank You that it is being done."*

God says in this regard:

> **For thus says the high and lofty One—He Who inhabits eternity, Whose name is Holy: I**

dwell in the high and holy place, but with him also who is of a thoroughly penitent and humble spirit, to revive the spirit of the humble and to revive the heart of the thoroughly penitent [bruised with sorrow for sin] (Isaiah 57:15 Amplified).

For all these things My hand has made, and so all these things have come into being [by and for Me], says the Lord. But this is the man to whom I will look and have regard: he who is humble and of a broken or wounded spirit, and who trembles at My word and reveres My commands (Isaiah 66:2 Amplified).

[For my determined purpose is] that I may know Him [that I may progressively become more deeply and intimately acquainted with Him, perceiving and recognizing and understanding the wonders of His Person more strongly and more clearly], and that I may in that same way come to know the power outflowing from His resurrection [which it exerts over believers], and that I may so share His sufferings as to be continually transformed [in spirit into His likeness even] to His death (Philippians 3:10 Amplified).

This, also, is the message of Romans 12:1-2. Let us look at it again:

"I beseech you therefore, brethren, by the mercies of God, that ye present your bodies a living sacrifice, holy, acceptable unto God, which is your reasonable service. And be not conformed to this world: but be ye transformed by the renewing of your mind, that ye may prove what is that good, and acceptable, and perfect, will of God."

This passage opens the door to hearing from God. It all begins by our pursuing Him. The end result of our pursuit is that He begins to transform us into His Image.

The tragedy is that the vast majority of all Christians will never know this wonderful victory in their lives. Their total experience with Christianity is having another individual tell them what to do in serving God. Yet God promises the Holy Spirit will guide them personally into all truth.

As stated earlier, babies cannot be led, they can only be fed. They can only handle milk in their helpless state of immaturity. Tragically, our churches have become daycare centers designed to entertain and perform while playing religious games. To keep the children of the babies interested, they take them to concerts and amusement parks rather than teach them meaty truth to live by. The power of God has left the church which has been now consigned to competing with the world. It has become an entertainment center rather than a house of prayer. As a result the poor helpless, hopeless Christians of today have lives and families devastated by satan!

The average baby believer does not understand his rights in Christ. He has been taught the new Christian psychology of defense rather than the Biblical position of offensive, aggressive warfare praying. What a pity! Satan was defeated at the cross by the blood of Jesus Christ. The believer need not ever be defeated.

Row, Row, Row Your Boat

I have preached the transformed life for many years. For the most part, very few Christians understand and practice the precious doctrine of the abundant life. The devil knows that if he can keep them in the "works of the flesh," they will never know God's personal will and direction. What's more, he doesn't have to worry about them when they pray. God says, *"Be ye transformed."* Satan says, "Do your best."

Religion, which satan authors and in which he operates, will often quote in error a familiar verse to confuse the carnal mind. It is, *"Faith without works is dead"* (James 2:17). The Amplified Bible gives a clearer picture of what God is saying in this verse:

So also faith if it does not have works (deeds and actions of obedience to back it up), by itself is destitute of power—inoperative, dead (James 2:17 Amplified).

Satan aims to guide you into a works mentality and will many times use this Scripture to position you in it.

Someone has given us an illustration of this kind of religious exercise that is contrary to biblical truth. According to the illustration, you get into a rowboat and have one oar marked "faith," and the other oar marked "'works." If you decided to live by faith alone, you would then put only the faith oar in the water and begin to pull. The result would be that you would go around in circles. Finding yourself going in a circle, you lay the faith oar down and then use just the works oar. Again, as a result, you still go in a circle. However, placing both the faith and works oars in the water and pulling together will put you on a straight line course.

"Well," you say, "Brother Bonner, that's good preaching. I like that. That sounds good to me—it must be what God had in mind, faith and works pulling together. One without the other is no good." No, my friend, that's bad doctrine. This is not God's will, nor is it the true meaning of the verse.

God says here that faith, the revelation of God's will within, will be visibly manifested through the believer as works. Faith is the mind of Christ. In essence, you're reaching for Him. Christ extends His mind into substance through you in response to your belief.

I am crucified with Christ: nevertheless I live; yet not I, but Christ liveth in me: and the life which I now live in the flesh I live by the faith of the Son of God, who loved me, and gave himself for me (Galatians 2:20).

Now faith is the substance of things hoped for, the evidence of things not seen (Hebrews 11:1).

When you understand the principle of *"faith without works is dead,"* it will tell you that you must, without hesitation, yield your life totally to Christ. From that place, He will then minister His life through yours.

You see, if the devil has to lose you to Jesus Christ through salvation, he will then try to get you to become physically active at being a Christian. Why? First, you must understand that laboring for Christ outside His will is *"sounding brass, tinkling cymbal," "wood, hay, stubble."* In other words, nothing. All true works are done through you by "prayers of faith" which result in the working of the Holy Spirit. You are first inwardly led of the Spirit. This brings the outward working of His will. Just doing things for God is useless and fruitless. It has no eternal significance. Second, be warned that this is satan's trap. He will see to it that you finally become weary in well doing. Through this, you will be easy to overcome with strongholds that strangle your Christian walk.

This is the falling away of this period of history spoken of in II Thessalonians 2:3:

"Let no man deceive you by any means: for that day shall not come, except there come a falling away first, and that man of sin be revealed, the son of perdition."

Satan makes you disillusioned, disappointed, discouraged, and then—the final snare—critical.

And the tongue is a fire, a world of iniquity: so is the tongue among our members, that it defileth the whole body, and setteth on fire the course of nature; and it is set on fire of hell. (James 3:6).

When he has consumed your confession, he has you totally bound and defeated.

For we all often stumble and fall and offend in many things. And if anyone does not offend

in speech [never says the wrong things], he is a fully developed character and a perfect man, able to control his whole body and to curb his entire nature. (James 3:2 Amplified).

Satan has to make you walk in the flesh. This is his turf. This is his territory of darkness. Once there, you will be totally disarmed and easily trapped and brought into defeat and bondage.

Labor void of God's will and power will eventually destroy all who desire to truly serve. It has no rewards but human recognition. This is why so many have fallen away from the Church today. There is no presence of God in their labor, therefore, it is just another job! Who wants something more to do when the television offers so much? Why waste a Sunday? Besides isn't it a day of rest? Going to church is work. Let the kids sleep. And in hell they lifted up their eyes . . .

Supernatural, Naturally

However, if you operate in a faith posture (hearing from God), your labor comes from your yieldedness to Christ and His ministry through you. The evident sign of that faith is the supernatural works of His will through your life. In essence, you live the supernatural, naturally.

This is what Romans 12:1 means when it says for this to happen you must "*. . . by the mercies of God. . . present your bodies.*" The imperative is that you commit yourself constantly back to God.

Again, the position of faith without works must be understood. If you say you have faith and God is not supernaturally moving through your life to perform that faith (His works), then you have dead faith. This means no faith at all. The evident sign of the "*faith of the Son of God*" is Christ performing His ministry through you.

I have been crucified with Christ [in Him I have shared His crucifixion]; it is no longer I

who live, but Christ (the Messiah) lives in me; and the life I now live in the body I live by faith in (by adherence to and reliance on and complete trust in) the Son of God, Who loved me and gave Himself up for me. (Galatians 2:20 Amplified).

So, therefore, works is a sign of faith—not our working, but God working through us in a supernatural way.

And what [is] the exceeding greatness of his power to us-ward who believe, according to the working of his mighty power (Ephesians 1:19).

Whereof I was made a minister, according to the gift of the grace of God given unto me by the effectual working of his power. (Ephesians 3:7).

Without it, we are as a ship with no power, dead in the water and subject to every storm of life.

Said in another way, you are to be constantly pursuing Jesus. You are to go after Christ with all of your being. This is also a sign of active faith. Please understand that we are told to go after Him over 100 times in the Bible. We are to hunger, thirst, seek, strain, pursue, chase, labor, violently assault the kingdom of God, etc. If you have been born again and truly seek His will, you will move your life constantly toward Him. You must pursue Him. You can do this by telling Him that you love Him. Openly praise the Lord with your lips. Love His Word and study it diligently. Abandon yourself to Him. Pray: "Lord, I agree with Your will for my life today." From that place of closeness to Him, you will then become sensitive to His voice intuitively. You will naturally (supernaturally) begin to experience the presence of the Lord.

I personally believe in and have experienced being able to hear from the Lord daily; He does speak to your spirit. Now, I'm not talking about an audible voice that comes from the mouth of God. I do not say that this could never happen, for the Bible records that it has happened in the past. What I am saying here is that because of constant yielding and growing, there can come a time in your daily walk when you become sensitive to God's mind and will for your life. You will know when God has spoken to you. He promises to "lead you into righteousness for His name's sake." His desire will ultimately become your desire; thereby, you will "walk in it." It can happen to you. Believe it and you will receive His will. This is God's greatest desire for the Christian's life.

However, to achieve it, He says that you must present your body a living (physically alive) sacrifice (soulishly dead) (Romans 12:1). This means dead to your own self (Galatians 2:20). It means to give up to Christ by reckoning in faith, "I am crucified, Lord; I yield my life to You." When a person dies, he is controlled by the will of the individual who picks him up. In a funeral, he is subject totally to those who are present to bury him. He has yielded without resistance or rebellion to their will alone. When you are dead to self you are totally abandoned to God's will alone. You have no will of your own.

As stated earlier, it is so tragic that the vast majority of all Christians will never walk at this level! They will enter Heaven someday having physically done their best for Jesus but having missed the supernatural life of the Spirit.

Altogether Vanity

Behold, thou hast made my days as an handbreadth; and mine age is as nothing before thee: verily every man at his best state is altogether vanity (Psalm 39:5).

I receive my best illustrations while preaching. Once, while ministering out of this Psalm, God opened the verse to me in an unusual way. It turned into an amusing declaration of its meaning. It went something like this: What is vanity? Well, you take a woman, give her $50 worth of facial make-up, set her in front of a mirror. In 30 minutes, she doesn't look the same, smell the same or act the same, and thank God for the difference. She has taken something that is and changed it into something that isn't, so when she gets around other isn'ts, they try to get her into the light to see how much "is" really is. They ask her what she is using and she lies and says, "Nothing." All the while, she's afraid of smiling lest her face crack. Then, when she gets home, she puts on fifty cents worth of cold cream and peels off all the paint. There "is" is, in all its shining glory, and she wonders why her husband turns off the light when he comes into the bedroom. Now, the point is, what is the table called that holds all of the products of hoped for beauty? It's called a "vanity."

Such is the work of the believer doing his "best" for Jesus. This is the Christian living in the state of fleshly works. That Christian will receive no reward other than having been born again. God's purpose for all who are physically born in history is that they be spiritually born again. However, if all they have at the judgment seat of Christ is just their works, this *"wood, hay, and stubble"* will all be burned by fire. They will receive no rewards. Nothing. Regardless, they will thank and praise God for their salvation and eternity in heaven, all the while lamenting what might have been if they would have obeyed Christ's deeper call.

It is so heartbreaking that this is the plight of the majority of all Christians. They remain for their entire Christian experience in the infant baby stage. That is, except on those occasions when tribulation drives them to deep prayer. From that place of momentary brokenness they experience for a season a total joyous commitment to Christ. During that short period of holding onto the Father, their prayers are answered due to their deep and desperate needs. They then spend the rest of their lives remembering and telling others of that short season of glory and intimacy with Christ.

In other words, in times of trouble, the religious

Christian gets serious (spiritual) with God. Therefore, he drives himself to the Lord and meets His condition for answered prayer. The trouble with this is, when God answers and the problem is resolved, satan moves quickly to blind the religious Christian's mind. He urgently works to hurry their retreat from this dangerous spiritual state of being in the will of God. The devil cannot control the believer who is totally given over to the Holy Spirit. Therefore, he works frantically by wiles (methods) to bring them back into fleshly worldliness and fear.

> **Put on God's whole armor [the armor of a heavy-armed soldier which God supplies], that you may be able successfully to stand up against [all] the strategies and the deceits of the devil (Ephesians 6:11 Amplified).**

How tragic to go through the Christian life with your spiritual eyes closed and stumbling from one day to the next! The result of all of this is that the "boat" goes in circles. It is a tragic waste and, what's more, totally unnecessary!

The Boat Goes Straight

We must submit totally and biblically to Jesus. His receiving us comes only through our desire and desperation. Only when we are broken can God bring to pass this wonderful experience of being one with Christ. This happens when we eagerly pursue the voice of His Spirit. As stated earlier, over 100 times in God's Word are we commanded to go after Him. Our commitment to this goal is the imperative of the faith walk. Physical labor is involved with any job. We must get up, get dressed, and go to work. In the same way, we get up in Christ, and we get dressed in Him (armor). Then, just as we extend the ideas and services of our employer, Christ works His will through us. Therein is faith and works together. Our faith produces His will and work through us. In the sea of God's will, the boat goes straight. It goes up and down many times, but always straight.

There is an old song that goes well here. It has meant much to my life. The title of it is *Stand By Me.*

> *When the storms of Life are raging,*
> *Stand by me.*
> *When the world is tossing me,*
> *Like a ship upon the sea,*
> *Thou who rulest wind and water,*
> *Stand by me.*
>   C. A. Tindley

God keeps the vessel straight.

Beloved, we must love Christ and search for Him with all of our hearts. We must present to Him every area of our lives. We must declare our desire to go on with an open heart. From the place of total abandonment you will begin to praise Him and to live for Him. In that process, you will develop a truly deeper relationship with Him. As a result, you will be led by the Spirit to study and meditate on Scripture verses in your mind. Eventually, the Word becomes His directing voice within. God states, *"Thy word have I hid in my heart that I may not sin against thee"* (Psalm 119:11). You will read and be quickened within by the Holy Spirit as He marries the power of the living Word of God to your spirit. Then you will begin to receive His personal plan and purpose for your own life. Once more, *"My sheep hear My voice."*

Holy Means Wholly

Delving deeper into this truth, Romans 12:1 reads: *"I beseech you therefore, brethren, by the mercies of God, that ye present your bodies a living sacrifice, holy . . . "* To understand the doctrine of presentation, you must realize you cannot serve God on your own terms (religion or works). You can serve Him on His terms only. He has set a specific standard for His will to begin working in your life.

Holiness does not come without "whollyness." Now, I

know there is no such word; however, it does describe this cardinal truth. To be holy as He is Holy, one must commit himself wholly to God. This is imperative if you are to hear within. God's price for His will in man's life is the constant yielding of all. In fact, the true measurement of holiness in the life of the Christian is the level that Christ completely controls. You are only as holy as He is Holy in you.

That doesn't mean that as of right now I can enter into His revealed will just by declaring, "God, I'll do anything You want me to do." To know the will of God, there must be continual, growing sanctity in your life. Holiness is not an experience, it is a Person. It is the person of Christ alive in you to the level of His reign and control. We are never to pursue the biblical principles of holiness and try to act them out. We are only to pursue Jesus. Then, He lives them through our lives. Our labor is to *"enter into rest"* as Hebrews 4 teaches. This brings the ceasing of the activity of law and the beginning of the ministry of grace.

Holiness, said another way, results from our yieldedness to Christ and His living His life through us. Our aggressive activity in Christian works is not the criteria of our actual walk in Him. However, Christ's activity through us is true holiness and produces the kingdom's work. Religious man says, as he studies Scripture, "Work for the night is coming." That in itself is true. However, man working in his own flesh will never produce Christ's will or life. Such a Christian operates only in religious activity. Men today futilely strive to build the church rather than the kingdom. Because of the powerless gospel there is, as God said in II Thessalonians 2:3, *"a falling away."*

Let no one deceive or beguile you in any way, for that day will not come except the apostasy comes first [unless the predicted great falling away of those who have professed to be Christians has come], and the man of lawlessness (sin) is revealed, who is the son of doom (of perdition) (II Thessalonians 2:3 Amplified).

Also, God calls the church of today *"lukewarm."*

> **So, because you are lukewarm and neither cold nor hot, I will spew you out of My mouth (Revelation 3:16 Amplified)!**

He knocks at the door and wants to come in and take over His people, but they won't let him.

> **Behold, I stand at the door and knock; if anyone hears and listens to and heeds My voice and opens the door, I will come in to him and will eat with him, and he [will eat] with Me (Revelation 3:20 Amplified).**

In this case, as always, the level of a man's faith will determine the level of Christ's control of his life (Galatians 2:20). Therefore, *"faith without works is dead."* Another way to say it: faith is the supernatural activity of Christ living through a person, performing His will. If there is no supernatural activity or results through an individual's life, then his works are the superficial works of the flesh. Revelation comes only by yielding your life to Christ. When you are living supernaturally (revelation) and not superficially (human effort), then His will is alive and active in you, and there are significant eternal results from your actions. Take the test. Are your works supernatural or superficial? Are you actually hearing from God?

Jesus said, *"I must work the works of Him who sent me."* We are to do the same, for as God extended His life through His Christ, so does Christ extend His life through us. This comes only by constantly committing everything you are to Him. We are told repetition is the greatest form of learning. Since the need for implanting these foundational principles into your mind is so desperate, I am going to continue to repeat them over and over in this writing. You must understand these critical truths to be able to discern the voice of God from the inside.

Finding God's will means going after Christ with all of

your heart, soul, and mind. It means pursuing Jesus Christ every moment in every matter until you are conditioned to His voice either through reading the Word or the Holy Spirit guiding from the inside to direct your steps.

This is the biblical condition the Holy Spirit lays out for the committed child of God to receive direction from Him. As you constantly yield your life, you will begin to receive the personal will of God.

> **Roll your works upon the Lord [commit and trust them wholly to Him; He will cause your thoughts to become agreeable to His will, and] so shall your plans be established and succeed (Proverbs 16:3 Amplified).**

> **I will give you the keys of the kingdom of heaven; and whatever you bind (declare to be improper and unlawful) on earth must be what is already bound in heaven; and whatever you loose (declare lawful) on earth must be what is already loosed in heaven (Matthew 16:19 Amplified).**

> **Truly I tell you, whatever you forbid and declare to be improper and unlawful on earth must be what is already forbidden in heaven, and whatever you permit and declare proper and lawful on earth must be what is already permitted in heaven. (Matthew 18:18 Amplified).**

As the will of God is increasingly received, you can actively, by obedience, give over to God's plan. From that point, you will continue by trusting (putting faith into) your revelation. Then, afterward, you must test what you hear within your spirit by the Scriptures. If you are constantly pursuing God, your inward judgements and inclinations will guide you, for the Holy Spirit *"will guide you into all truth" (John 16:13).*

Inspiration, Not Perspiration

A good rule of thumb when walking with the Lord is, if

you encounter doubt in a situation—don't. Cease immediately the direction you are going and begin to pray. If what you are doing is of God, assurance will overwhelmingly return to your spirit as His will. If it is not, you will feel a release of burden or second thoughts about your intentions. In fact, if you think you are walking in the light but within you that light starts to dim, immediately stop heading in that direction. No matter how it hurts your pride, admit you're wrong. Turn and go back to where you compromised. You do this by confession and true repentance. Then wait patiently and prayerfully for His light to return.

If we [freely] admit that we have sinned and confess our sins, He is faithful and just (true to His own nature and promises) and will forgive our sins [dismiss our lawlessness] and [continuously] cleanse us from all unrighteousness [everything not in conformity to His will in purpose, thought, and action] (I John 1:9 Amplified).

From there, praise Him until joy again fills your heart. In doing so, you will reestablish the "walk" and His close presence within.

Remember that *"God is light"* and, as light, He is in constant motion. For the believer to seek focus, he must constantly pursue Him. Christ has a path for your life. It is a directed path. In fact, every day, He brings His will to your life.

For we are his workmanship, created in Christ Jesus unto good works, which God hath before ordained that we should walk in them (Ephesians 2:10).

Another Scripture that emphasizes this is found in Job 7:17-18:

What is man, that thou shouldest magnify him? and that thou shouldest set thine heart upon him? And that thou shouldest visit him every morning, and try him every moment?

The heart of God is His will. Your responsibility is to seek Him and yield completely to His will. Even if it means a total and immediate change in your ambitions or lifestyle, you must go back to where you left Him. You must do it and, believe me, it is wonderfully worth it! This is the only place of obedience. Christ Jesus did not leave you; you left Him and stumbled into darkness. He does not follow, He only leads.

Let us again look to the Word to understand how God produces His holiness in the Christian's life. First, *"God is light and in Him there is no darkness at all"* (I John 1:5). When we pursue God, we go after the "light." Here we must understand that satan is the counterfeit light and has with him in his service, demons masquerading as angels of light.

For such [are] false apostles, deceitful workers, transforming themselves into the apostles of Christ. And no marvel; for Satan himself is transformed into an angel of light (II Corinthians 11:13-14).

This is why we must be able to discern within by the power of the Holy Spirit that which is of God and that which is of the devil. Both God and satan operate in the area of our feelings. God's Spirit speaks to man's spirit; satan speaks to the soul-flesh of man. To discern the difference, the Christian must grow and mature. A true disciple must move from feelings to faith. How important this is for the Christian to understand and comprehend! The Lord reveals His light by inspiration—not by perspiration. Remember that only when there is inspiration (revelation), do we receive the capacity and potential to do the works of God!

As stated earlier, holiness is not an experience, it is a Person: the Person of Christ alive in us. Only this kind of holiness will meet the Father's standards and make our lives pleasing and acceptable in His sight (Romans 12:1).

Be All You Can Be

The Lord concludes this verse with *"which is your*

reasonable service." Here Paul, who has begged the Roman Church to give all over to Christ, finishes the statement with this admonition. He knows if they give all over to Jesus Christ the Holy Spirit will reveal to them all that Christ is and all that He has done for them in His life, death, and resurrection. He wants to embed this truth beyond their finite, human minds into their spirit man. Only God can reveal Himself to man and has a standard for the way He does it.

At the time of this writing, the government is using a special slogan to induce young people to join the military. They call upon them to "Be all that you can be." This says to those interested that there is an incredible future in becoming a part of the U.S. Army. Such is Paul's begging the Romans to get into the place where they can experience the voice of God in their spirit. From that position, the Holy Spirit can explode truth in their beings to produce Christ's life within. Such wondrous tasting of the Father's goodness (I Peter 2:3) would propel them to give everything over to God—their body, spirit, mind, emotion and will. This position of blessing comes not by the effort of flesh, but by the joyous yielding of all you are and hope to be. In essence, the Lord is saying that, to be all you can be, you must present yourself totally to Him. God's Word declares:

For we are God's own handiwork (His workmanship), recreated in Christ Jesus (born anew), that we may do those good works which God predestined (planned beforehand) for us, (taking paths which He prepared ahead of time) that we should walk in them—living the good life which He prearranged and made ready for us to live" (Ephesians 2:10, Amplified).

This Scripture, proclaims that we are God's handiwork. What we are and all the abilities we have belong to Him. He made us. All that is, is His. Not only that, but He also has a path (His will) for us to pursue and on which to constantly place ourselves. The choice is ours—death or life, darkness or light, works or grace, flesh or faith, self or Christ! We will go deeper with these truths in this book. It is something every Christian must understand. Without it, there is no hearing within.

Good Gifts from God

Many of us who have spent a lifetime in study of the "Lordship" doctrine have been drawn to the writings of Oswald Chambers. We have experienced in the journals of his Christian journey a complete abandonment of his life to Christ. His writings speak of a oneness with the Holy Spirit. In his life, we again see that coming to the hearing place with God was only achieved by desperation. Hear him as he tells his own story of being introduced to the Holy Spirit.

> I was in Dunoon College as a tutor in philosophy, when Dr. F. B. Meyer came and spoke about the Holy Spirit. I determined to have all that was going, and went to my room and asked God simply and definitely for the baptism of the Holy Spirit, whatever that meant. From that day on for four years, nothing but the overruling grace of God and kindness of friends kept me out of an asylum.
>
> God used me during those years for the conversion of souls, but I had no conscious communion with Him. The Bible was the dullest, most uninteresting book in existence, and the sense of depravity, the vileness and bad-motivedness of my nature, was terrific. I see now that God was taking me by the light of the Holy Spirit and His Word through every ramification of my being.
>
> The last three months of those years things reached a climax. I was getting very desperate. I knew no one who had what I wanted; in fact I did not know what I did want. But I knew that if what I had was all the Christianity there was, the thing was a fraud. Then Luke 11:13 got hold of me — *"If ye then, being evil, know how to give good gifts to your children, how much more shall your heavenly*

Father give the Holy Spirit to them that ask Him?"

But how could I, bad motivated as I was, possibly ask for the gift of the Holy Spirit? Then it was borne in upon me that I had to claim the gift from God on the authority of Jesus Christ and testify to having done so. But the thought came—if you claim the gift of the Holy Spirit on the word of Jesus Christ and testify to it, God will make it known to those who know you best how bad you are in heart. And I was not willing to be a fool for Christ's sake. But those of you who know the experience, know very well how God brings one to the point of utter despair, and I got to the place where I did not care whether everyone knew how bad I was; I cared for nothing on earth, saving to get out of my present condition.

At a little meeting held during a mission in Dunoon, a well known lady was asked to take the after meeting. She did not speak, but set us to prayer, and then sang "Touch me again, Lord." I felt nothing, but I knew emphatically my time had come, and I rose to my feet. I had no vision of God, only a sheer dogged determination to take God at His word and to prove this thing for myself, and I stood up and said so.

That was bad enough, but what followed was ten times worse. After I had sat down the lady worker, who knew me well, said: "That is very good of our brother, he has spoken like that as an example to the rest of you."

Up I got again and said: "I got up for no one (else's) sake, I got up for my own sake; either Christianity is a downright fraud, or I have not got hold of the right end of the stick." And then and there I claimed the gift of the Holy Spirit in dogged committal on Luke 11:13.

I had no vision of heaven or of angels, I had nothing. I was as dry and empty as ever, no power or realization of God, no witness of the Holy Spirit. Then I was asked to speak at a meeting and forty souls came out to the front. Did I praise God? No, I was terrified and left them to the workers, and went to Mr. MacGregor (a friend) and told him what had happened, and he said: "Don't you remember claiming the Holy Spirit as a gift on the word of Jesus, and that He said; *Ye shall receive power?*' This is the power from on high." Then like a flash something happened inside me, and I saw that I had been wanting power in my own hand, so to speak, that I might say, "Look what I have by putting my all on the altar."

If the four previous years had been hell on earth, these last five years have truly been heaven on earth. Glory be to God, the last aching abyss of the human heart is filled to overflowing with the love of God. Love is the beginning, love is the middle and love is the end. After He comes in, all you see is "Jesus only, Jesus ever."

When you know what God has done for you, the power and the tyranny of sin are gone and the radiant, unspeakable emancipation of the indwelling Christ has come, and when you see men and women who should be princes and princesses with God bound up by the show of things—oh, you begin to understand what the Apostle meant when he said he wished himself accursed from Christ that men might be saved! (Edman)

Oswald Chamber's experience of the baptism of the Holy Spirit was different than that of Charles Finney described in the Appendix. Finney's baptism was accomplished in a few days. The process for Chambers took four years. Finney experienced the conscious presence of God while Chambers felt nothing while standing on the promise of God. Finney knew what had happened immediately, while Chambers didn't even know he had received the Holy Spirit until His power was revealed through his life. Both experiences, however, were just as real and the results just as profound. Each is a demonstration of the consuming power of the indwelling Holy Spirit in the life of a believer who is submitted to God.

Chambers experienced God in fullness. He tasted the total leading of God's Holy Spirit. Still today, believers are blessed and filled through the revelations that God gave him within. In almost every Christian home, you will find his book *My Utmost for His Highest*. He was the epitome of the meaning of Luke 11:13:

If ye then, being evil, know how to give good gifts unto your children: how much more shall your heavenly Father give the Holy Spirit to them that ask him?

You will ask me, "Are you satisfied? Have you got all you want?" God forbid. With the deepest feeling of my soul I can say that I am satisfied with Jesus now; but there is also the consciousness of how much fuller the revelation can be of the exceeding abundance of His grace. Let us never hesitate to say, "This is only the beginning" When we are brought into the holiest of all, we are only beginning to take our right position with the Father. I have learnt to place myself before God every day, as a vessel to be filled with His Holy Spirit. He has filled me with the blessed assurance that He, as the everlasting God, has guaranteed His work in me.

— Andrew Murray

Chapter Four

Walking in the Light

Take a deeper look at Ephesians 2:10. God revealed to me through Bible study a number of years ago that He had a daily path laid out before me. At the beginning of the day (the moment I awaken) I choose, in prayer, to place my life in His kingdom and will.

> **And if it seem evil unto you to serve the LORD, choose you this day whom ye will serve; whether the gods which your fathers served that [were] on the other side of the flood, or the gods of the Amorites, in whose land ye dwell: but as for me and my house, we will serve the LORD (Joshua 24:15).**

The Scripture teaches the pathway laid out is already illumined as the Word within is the *"light to my path, the lamp to my feet"* (Psalm 119:105). As I begin the journey in obedience to His will, I follow as the light begins to move. This is His will in action through my life. My part in this relationship is to stay constantly focused on and in that moving light through my desire to obey. The doctrinal basis for this action is God's Biblical admonitions to *"Put on,"* *"Stand fast,"* *"Take unto,"* *"Be ye,"* *"Let this mind,"* *"Blessed are,"* *"Take up,"* etc. All of these admonitions are for our instruction (by inward desire and pursuit) to go after Him constantly. Again, He tells us to walk in the light, as He is in the light.

> **But if we [really] are living and walking in the Light, as He [Himself] is in the Light, we have [true, unbroken] fellowship with one another, and the blood of Jesus Christ His Son cleanses (removes) us from all sin and guilt [keeps us cleansed from sin in all its forms and manifestations] (I John 1:7 Amplified).**

Just as the light is always in motion, so is the will of God. We must constantly seek after it. We must go to Him. Satan cannot hit a moving target, nor one that is covered with light. His arrows of doubt and accusations are shafts of darkness that instantly dissolve when they come in contact with the illuminating armor that is our covering.

With this thought in mind and because God has given you a wonderful opportunity to truly live in Him, I urge you to lay aside every weight and sin that so easily besets you. Overcome all feelings of resentment and unforgiveness. You can experience true life and joy only in the center of God's will. It is impossible to engage in both inward (spirit-led) and outward (religion-led) activities. In this case, one is oil and the other is water. They will not mix. The internal experience of being led of the Spirit is, as stated earlier, the "abundant life," or Christ's life through us.

The external doings are the works of the flesh, or religion. Satan plans, through flesh works, to destroy the will and purpose of God. This is the business of Abaddon (satan) the destroyer.

> **Over them as king they have the angel of the Abyss (of the bottomless pit). In Hebrew his name is Abbaddon [destruction], but in**

Greek he is called Apollyon [destroyer] (Revelation 9:11 Amplified).

As we have said time and again, God is constantly up to something in your life. Therefore, for Him to become active, you must join yourself to His life. This action begins with you! Christ's life will not operate through our lives based on the ministry we desire. Our lives must operate by His life in our obedience.

This is not to say that God will not anoint what you are already doing at the time you become one with Him: God's ways are not our ways. However, when He becomes Himself in us, He overwhelms us, first with His glory, and then with His marvelous faith and works of grace. Oh, the joy of being one with Christ! I can say without hesitation that the greatest times of your life will be in His will.

I was not born again until I was twenty-three. Regardless of this, I had known all of my young life, as a child and a teenager, that someday I would preach the Gospel. God's call comes from before the foundation of the world. In many cases, what a person is doing before total submission could be God's calling in his life to prepare him to hear.

For he who has once entered [God's] rest also has ceased from [the weariness and pain] of human labors, just as God rested from those labors peculiarly His own (Hebrews 4:10 Amplified).

If our labor does not produce the rest of God, then the Lord will prune our flesh activity away.

I AM the True Vine, and My Father is the Vinedresser. Any branch in Me that does not bear fruit [that stops bearing] He cuts away (trims of, takes away); and He cleanses and repeatedly prunes every branch that continues to bear fruit, to make it bear more and richer and more excellent fruit. You are cleansed and pruned already, because of the

word which I have given you [the teachings I have discussed with you]. Dwell in Me, and I will dwell in you. [Live in Me, and I will live in you.] Just as no branch can bear fruit of itself without abiding in (being vitally united to) the vine, neither can you bear fruit unless you abide in Me. I am the Vine; you are the branches. Whoever lives in Me and I in him bears much (abundant) fruit. However, apart from Me [cut off from vital union with Me] you can do nothing. If a person does not dwell in Me, he is thrown out like a [broken-off] branch, and withers; such branches are gathered up and thrown into the fire, and they are burned. If you live in Me [abide vitally united to Me] and My words remain in you and continue to live in your hearts, ask whatever you will, and it shall be done for you. When you bear (produce) much fruit, My Father is honored and glorified, and you show and prove yourselves to be true followers of Mine. (John 15:1-8 Amplified).

Believe me, prune He will.

Running Over

When something is filled to running over, that which enters within it covers it completely. When it is totally inundated, it then becomes one with it, much as flowing water does when it fills a glass to capacity. As the water begins cascading over the vessel, you then observe only the liquid. If the glass underneath is clear, it becomes totally invisible.

God says: *"And be not drunk with wine, wherein is excess; but be ye filled with the Spirit"* (Ephesians 5:18). The filling of the Spirit here is a direct command of God. You must commit to Him everything that you are for this to happen. You must go after the light and choose to remain within its perimeter. When you do so, you live in God's volitional, as well as His operational, will. You say, "Oh, yes, that is my desire. How do I accomplish that?" By constantly staying your mind upon Him.

> **Let this same attitude and purpose and
> [humble] mind be in you which was in Christ
> Jesus: [Let Him be your example in humility:]
> (Philippians 2:5 Amplified).**

Then you will become what you already are from the
moment of salvation: crucified (Galatians 2:20). From that
position, desire with all of your heart to be filled and to
operate in the resurrected life. You will then realize and
begin to experience God's daily plan as it is already working in you as a born again Christian. It is there waiting to
become active as you choose to let it.

> **But the fruit of the [Holy] Spirit [the work
> which His presence within accomplishes] is
> love, joy (gladness), peace, patience (an even
> temper, forbearance), kindness, goodness
> (benevolence), faithfulness; (Meekness, humil-
> ity) gentleness, self-control (self-restraint,
> continence). Against such things there is no
> law [that can bring a charge]. And those who
> belong to Christ Jesus, the Messiah, have cru-
> cified the flesh—the Godless human nature—
> with its passions and appetites and desires. If
> we live by the (Holy) Spirit, let us also walk by
> the Spirit.—If by the (Holy) Spirit we have our
> life [in God], let us go forward walking in line,
> our conduct controlled by the Spirit.
> (Galatians 5:22-25 Amplified).**

To bring this to pass in your life, you must give yourself
totally over to Christ as an act of your will. You must desperately desire to be filled. The end results are as He has
promised, He pours Himself into and over your life. Then
He begins His work through you. As we stated earlier, it is
so tragic that very few ever come into this wondrous place
with Christ.

Satan desperately works to blind Christians to this
truth. He must. He covers his system with darkness. Christ
covers His World in light. Satan knows he cannot control a
broken believer. He accomplishes control through the
binding power of unforgiveness, lust, or wiles. When

he captures believers, they spend their born again lives begging God for the help that is already theirs to act on. Their infant state blinds them to His help. It is like what happens when a baby crawls onto a heated floor vent and begins to burn. Its reaction is to sit down as it screams for help, when in reality it could crawl off of it.

Beloved, at salvation, we are already crucified. God places His resurrection power in us at the moment of our new birth. It comes in with the Holy Spirit. Therefore, we must act from that position. Let me give you an example. I am Mickey Bonner for my lifetime. I don't have to do anything to be that. I am he—warts, ugliness, and all. I just need to overcome my pride and insecurities and be me. This is the same way with the spirit-filled life. Just allow Christ to be Himself in you. Abandon to Him. Fight to be filled. Confess, forgive, make restitution. Do anything God says to your heart to be filled and operate in His Spirit. When that happens, you will discover He's already working in you.

> **"Having made known unto us the mystery of His will, according to his good pleasure which he hath purposed in himself."** **(Ephesians 1:9)**

> **"For it is God which worketh in you both to will and to do of his good pleasure." (Philippians 2:13).**

> **"Wherefore also we pray always for you, that our God would count you worthy of this calling, and fulfill all the good pleasure of his goodness, and the work of faith with power." (II Thessalonians 1:11)**

To say it another way—if you are saved, become what you already are. Satan will attempt to destroy your victory with negative accusations. Nevertheless, as you actively become what you already are in Him, you let the precious Spirit of Christ manifest Himself to and through your life. This process produces the will of God living through you. For, you see, "to present yourself" means you are constantly presenting your life to Christ. With this comes transformation. This is God's part.

P/T = GW

The equation for this would be, *"presentation over transformation equals God's will,"* or *"P/T = GW."* The lost world and carnal Christians cannot understand this formula. If used in one totally committed life, this formula could change the world. It is the *"humble themselves"* of II Chronicles 7:14.

If My people, who are called by My name, shall humble themselves, pray, seek, crave, and require of necessity My face and turn from their wicked ways, then will I hear from Heaven, forgive their sin, and heal their land (II Chronicles 7:14 Amplified).

With this thought in mind, let's take another look at James 2:17: *"Even so faith, if it hath not works, is dead, being alone."* In this unique statement, the Spirit tells us that true works are God's flow to and through us. God has the plan and the power to implement them if we supply the faith from within to make it work. Another way of saying it is, the level of one's faith is the level of Christ's control in the Christian life. Our level of faith (our pursuit and walk with and of God) will equal the standard of maturity essential to being able to hear a word from God in our spirit man. From there, we act on that which we cannot see with our eyes, but receive within our minds a word from God according to Hebrews 11:1: *"Now faith is the substance of things hoped for, the evidence of things not seen."*

Pursuing Christ starts the process of "growing in grace" where we can begin to see, and then comprehend. Then, with the eyes of Christ, we see what His will is as He reveals it to us with heavenly vision. From there, He enables us within to believe Him for it to happen. This is the total message of Hebrews 11. Though they did not see with their eyes, they all received the "report" when they prayed. Herein, they knew it was done before it was done;

therefore, it was done! And, beloved, two thousand years after Hebrews was written, *it still works*, or better said, *He still works through us*.

Your abandonment of self-will to follow His will allows Him to begin to speak to your mind. This is the *"renewing of your mind"* of Romans 12:2. From here, the transformation begins. When we become *"a living sacrifice"* (our overwhelming desire to walk with Him), we then move ourselves into God's part of His divine plan (Romans 12:1-2). The act of volitional choice begins with us. Hence, verse one demands total commitment. From there, verse two reads: *"And be ye not conformed to this world: but be ye transformed by the renewing of your mind."* Verse one is our part, based on God's demand for total commitment; verse two is God's part, in response to our yieldedness. It is His mind and His will working through us. It is the beginning of the greatest experience a person will ever know. Oh, to be His, crucified, resurrected and ministering His will. What joy floods the soul!

All true ministry from God can be only on His level. God is our Father. His ways are not our ways. He is so far beyond us that He must do a growing work within our spirit just so we can begin to comprehend.

Because God speaks so much of us as childlike, I would bring again an illustration using our baby state. We would be like an infant riding with its parents on a jet airliner. It comprehends at its level of reasoning the noise, the atmosphere and parental care. No other capabilities lie within its level of maturity. Then, after it grows and matures through the study and experience, that same infant could someday do the work of the pilot. He will, by the process of maturing, become knowledgeable of all the instruments, conditions and the judgment to operate the same aircraft. We all began as *"babes in Christ."*

However, Brethren, I could not talk to you as to spiritual [men], but as to nonspiritual [men of the flesh, in whom the carnal nature predominates], as to mere infants [in the new life] in Christ [unable to talk yet!] (I Corinthians 3:1 Amplified).

The catastrophe is most Christians stay that way.

The Wonder of It All

For us to even begin to enter into this state, we must present ourselves holy by His standards through His life within.

> **I beseech you therefore, brethren, by the mercies of God, that ye present your bodies a living sacrifice, holy, acceptable unto God, which is your reasonable service. (Romans 12:1).**

Then, He—by a miracle act—transforms us so we understand and do His will.

> **And be not conformed to this world: but be ye transformed by the renewing of your mind, that ye may prove what is that good, and acceptable, and perfect, will of God (Romans 12:2).**

The word transformed here is from the Greek word for metamorphosis. The best illustration of this word is the phenomenon that happens to a caterpillar when it goes into the cocoon cycle and emerges as a new life form—a butterfly. In its first stage, it is a ground-bound crawler. In its second stage, it becomes a free form with the mental and physical dimension of flight as its new lifestyle. What an incredible transformation. In its prior state it spent its life trying to keep from being stepped on. Then, in its state of translation it becomes free and flies above the elements. This is the true meaning of living from glory to glory.

> **Let no person deceive himself. If anyone among you supposes that he is wise in this age, let him become a fool [let him discard his worldly discernment and recognize himself as dull, stupid, and foolish, without true learning and scholarship], that he may become [really] wise (I Corinthians 3:18 Amplified).**

Thus is the Christian who in constant pursuit abandons his life to Christ. The Holy Spirit enters into him and reprograms his total mind and lifestyle. Then, as the believer constantly gives his life back to Christ daily, God continues to reveal Himself to the individual. Through this process, God continually changes him. As a result He produces to and through him the life of Christ here on this earth.

For [as far as this world is concerned] you have died, and your [new, real] life is hidden with Christ in God (Colossians 3:3 Amplified).

To reach this wondrous level, you must desire deeply and act constantly to present your body and life to God. With this comes the transformation and revelation of the mind of Christ. "Oh," you say, "Brother Bonner, I desire deeply to know the mind of God. In fact, I want more than anything else to know His will for my own personal life. How can it be done?"

To say it again, you discover His will only by constantly presenting your life totally at the level of God's acceptance. You enter into His presence (mind) at the level of your maturity. You can do this if you desire Him with all of your heart. You have nothing to give to God but yourself. This is all He wants. Once you abandon yourself to Him, He begins to develop His will and purpose through you. The end result is your finding out who you really are by finding out who He is in you. From there, you begin the glorious transition into His world. As the old song says, "Oh, the wonder of it all."

Incredible Journey

God teaches this principle in many ways throughout Scripture. For instance, consider the teaching of the Vine found in John 15. When you are born again, you immediately become one with Christ. That is salvation. But in order to grow, you must constantly reach for the Vine (Jesus) and hold on, engrafted into it! This is your part.

The word God uses here is *"abide,"* or your willingness to

stay and go on. As you labor to be in the Vine's life, growth and transformation come. Finally in this relationship, the *"fruit of the Vine"* begins to show through your life. The fruit is Christ producing Himself through you. In this regard, the Scripture states, *"Blessed are they that hunger and thirst after righteousness, for they shall be filled" (Matthew 5:6).* Now, the words hunger and thirst mean an unquenchable desire to become a part of and alive with Jesus Christ.

Once engrafted in and captured by the Holy Spirit, you love Him more than you love yourself. At this point, the Holy Spirit will bring the child of God into the greatest relationship to life he has ever known. He will then become what God intended for him to become. It is just the beginning of a journey that has no ending. In fact, this life journey constantly increases in dimension beyond description. I do not care who you are and what your present circumstances; if you will give your total life over to God continually, it will be the beginning of an incredible journey. It will be the beginning of life as God knows it and speaks of in His Word. You can choose to start at this moment.

Andrew Murray (P/T = GW)

The story of Andrew Murray, the great saint of God whose writings have blessed the saints for over a hundred years, illustrates this point. He had been an ordained clergyman for ten years, yet he felt that there was no power or fulfillment in his life or ministry. He sought a fuller realization of sanctification in his life. He wanted to experience true holiness. He described his situation and experience in these words:

> Though all around thought me one of the most earnest of men, my life was one of deep dissatisfaction. I struggled and prayed as best I could. One day I was talking with a missionary. I do not think he knew much of the power of sanctification himself-he would have admitted it. When we were talking and he saw my earnestness, he said, "Brother, remember that when God puts a desire into your heart, He will fulfill it." That helped me; I thought of it a

hundred times. I want to say the same to you, who are plunging about and struggling in the quagmire of helplessness and doubt. The desire that God puts into your heart, He will fulfill.

Well, God helped me, and for seven or eight years I went on, always inquiring and seeking, and always getting. Then came, about 1870, the great Holiness Movement. The letters that appeared in *The Revival* touched my heart; and I was in close fellowship with what took place at Oxford and Brighton, and it all helped me. Perhaps if I were to talk of consecration I might tell you of an evening there in my own study in Cape Town. Yet I cannot say that that was my deliverance, for I was still struggling. Later on, my mind became much exercised about the baptism of the Holy Spirit, and I gave myself to God as perfectly as I could to receive the baptism of the Spirit. Yet there was failure; God forgive it. It was somehow as if I could not get what I wanted. Through all these stumblings God led me, without any very special experience that I can point to; but as I look back I do believe now that He was giving me more and more of His blessed Spirit, had I but known it better.

I can help you more, perhaps, by speaking, not of any marked experience, but by telling very simply what I think God has given me now, in contrast to the first ten years of my Christian life. *In the first place, I have learnt to place myself before God every day, as a vessel to be filled with His Holy Spirit. He has filled me with the blessed assurance that He, as the everlasting God, has guaranteed His work in me.* If there is one lesson that I am learning day by day, it is this: that it is God who worketh all in all. Oh, that I could help any brother or sister to realize this!

You will ask me, "Are you satisfied? Have you got all you want?" God forbid. With the deepest feeling of my soul I can say that I am satisfied with Jesus now; but there is also the consciousness of how much fuller the revelation can be of the exceeding abundance of His grace. Let us never hesitate to say, "This is only the beginning." When we are brought into the holiest of all, we are only beginning to take our right position with the Father. (Edman, emphasis added)

Here in a nutshell is the essence of hearing from God. First, God was calling Murray as an immature Christian to deeper relationship with Himself. Like the baby on a jetliner, Murray did not fully comprehend what God was doing, but the strong desire for sanctification was a call from God in Murray's life. But it did not stop there. Murray went on with God, pressing his life toward the Master into an ever purer and fuller walk with Him. He earnestly struggled to comprehend the meaning of consecration and the baptism of the Holy Spirit. Next, he reached the place where he presented his life to God every day to be filled with His Holy Spirit (presentation (P)). His life and mind were transformed and renewed daily (transformation (T)). He was filled with the assurance that God had "guaranteed His work in Him" (God's will (GW)). Murray was attached to the Vine and its life was flowing through him. Finally, he lived in deep satisfaction flowing from his relationship with Jesus, yet conscious of the fact that it is only the beginning, as he sought a fuller revelation of the abundance of His grace. What a glorious experience!

Is God any different today than in Andrew Murray's day? I think not. If you have a yearning to know God better and to hear His voice more clearly, who do you think put that desire in your heart? It was certainly not the devil and your flesh will not manufacture such a desire on its own. What the missionary said to Murray is just as true for you. "When God puts a desire in your heart, He will fulfill it." But you must go on with God, pressing your life to Him daily; making strides, then stumbling; experiencing victory and failure, yet drawing ever closer to a holy God; staying attached to the Vine so that its life is expressed through you in ever increasing measure. In the middle of this process, you find that you begin to know the mind and will of the Father as He "guarantees His work in you." Hallelujah!

Let's Have Fun

To truly focus in on this truth, let's look back again to

Romans 12:2, where God says *"Be ye not conformed to this world."* First, you must understand what *"world"* means. At the time Paul wrote this epistle, Christians still sought to mingle law and grace to prove their Christianity. They had walked in religion for centuries by keeping the Old Testament procedures as a part of their salvation and lifestyle. Paul knew this when he told them not to "be conformed," for in doing so, they were falling back to a law position. To prove their new birth and Christian status, they would add to the grace act of salvation by circumcising their children. They had reverted back to religion by adding works to God's marvelous grace. This, of course, was foolish. It is not the circumcision of the flesh but the cutting away of the old man by the Holy Spirit within that established the foundation of salvation.

But he is a Jew who is one inwardly, and [true] circumcision is of the heart, a spiritual and not a literal [matter]. His praise is not from men but from God (Romans 2:29 Amplified).

This begins the moment one gives his life to God through Christ. Then, as the believer begins to grow in Him, the Lord (by the Holy Spirit) surgically removes from his being the hatred, lust, unforgiveness, etc. His invisible working within the growing Christian will cause him to begin to *"lay aside every weight and the sin which doth so easily beset [him]"* (Hebrews 12:1).

The more weight a runner carries, the less speed and less distance the runner is capable of. This is being conformed to the world. What then are the weights in the modern church? One is a Christian operating in the activity of his flesh without prayer and trying to be spiritual based on man's programs. He is performing religious activity. You say, "What then is being spiritual, if it is not works?" As stated earlier in several ways, it is the individual Christian reckoning himself crucified and then pursuing Jesus by making Christ the daily priority of his life.

I am crucified with Christ: nevertheless I live; yet not I, but Christ liveth in me: and the

life which I now live in the flesh I live by the faith of the Son of God, who loved me, and gave himself for me (Galatians 2:20).

No carnal Christian will ever know the personal will of God in his life, nor will he know His revelation, or even His mind. There can be no real intercession until one has pursued Jesus to such a place that there is nothing left in his heart but Him. One must seek after Him with all of his spirit, soul and body. The Christian must put Christ first before family, job, or his own individual life. When he does this, then real life begins and the Holy Spirit places all of the things of the past in divine order. Incidentally, when you have reached this place of growth, God will, through you, bring joy to your family, direction in your employment, and victory to your own soul.

You might ask, "Is there any fun in that kind of life?" Yes, there is. The only real fun you will ever know is in that wondrous experience. I use the word "fun" here loosely, for in reality it is a place of unspeakable joy and perfect peace and rest. In fact, the only time you will ever touch completeness will be in the total commitment of your life to Christ. In the course of this, you will experience His personal will for you. It all begins with "presentation." Better said, your life truly begins when you choose to give yourself over to God's perfect plan by accepting the will of the Savior regardless of His intentions.

You must accept that God has a daily personal plan and path for your life. In order to present yourself for His transformation, you must say, in faith, from your heart, "All right, Lord, regardless of what it is, I desire it. Regardless of what You want, I'm going to do it. I joyfully yield; expectantly wait. It means everything to me to be in Your personal will. I submit; I surrender; I commit my life to You. I am crucified."

Consider one final word on this matter of presentation for transformation. We humans are the presentation of God, in that God made man and put him in the world. In fact, all human flesh belongs totally to Him.

And the LORD God formed man [of] the

dust of the ground, and breathed into his nostrils the breath of life; and man became a living soul (Genesis 2:7).

We find in the Bible that God is the creator of all. He made the world for man and then He made man out of the world (dust of the ground). He gave him a soul and spirit that man might, by his own choice of will, repent of his sins, chose God, and receive the work of His Son on the cross. When we trust Christ in true salvation, we then become the habitation of God.

No man has at any time [yet] seen God. But if we love one another, God abides (lives and remains) in us and His love [that love which is essentially His] is brought to completion—to its full maturity, runs its full course, is perfected—in us! By this we come to know (perceive, recognize and understand) that we abide (live and remain) in Him and He in us: because He has given (imparted) to us of His (Holy) Spirit (1 John 4:12-13, Amplified).

At the moment of your salvation, you are the liberation of God. *"If the Son, therefore, shall make you free, ye shall be free indeed"* (John 8:36). When you have pursued Christ with all of your heart to the filling of the Spirit, you will have then presented your life to Christ. From this position, God declares, *"Herein is my Father glorified, that ye bear much fruit; so shall ye be my disciples"* (John 15:8). Incidentally, as stated earlier, the fruit of a Christian is not another Christian, it is Jesus producing His life through them. This is the true fruit of the vine.

One of the greatest examples of the committed life was Hudson Taylor. He was a man of answered prayer. He was born again in his early years. As a young man, he felt God's call to the mission field in China. There he served for fifteen years by the strength of the flesh. He desired to go on with God but had not found the key that unlocks the door to holiness. In the midst of his inner conflicts, he penned a letter to his mother explaining his desire to know the fullness of God. He wrote:

My own position becomes continually more and more responsible, and my need greater of special grace to fill it; but I have continually to mourn that I follow at such a distance and learn so slowly to imitate my precious Master. I cannot tell you how I am buffeted sometimes by temptation. I never knew how bad a heart I had. Yet I do know that I love God and love His work, and desire to serve Him only in all things. And I value above all things that precious Saviour in Whom alone I can be accepted. Often I am tempted to think that one so full of sin cannot be a child of God at all; but I try to throw it back, and rejoice all the more in the preciousness of Jesus, and in the riches of that grace that has made us accepted in the Beloved. Beloved He is of God; beloved He ought to be of us. But oh, how short I fall here again! May God help me to love Him more and serve Him better. Do pray for me. Pray that the Lord will keep me from sin, will sanctify me wholly, will use me more largely in His service. (Edman)

Though he struggled, Hudson Taylor's heart was totally turned to God. He desired with all his being to know the fullness of God's grace and power. By his own effort, he could not find the way. It is always God's plan to create hunger and then fill it. Thus He did in this hungry man. As Taylor experienced his greatest brokenness, God answered him through a letter from a fellow missionary, John McCarthy. The letter contained a road map to the freedom he so sought. Thus was Hudson Taylor liberated into the Vine-life of Christ through him. McCarthy wrote:

To let my loving Saviour work in me His will, my sanctification is what I would live for by His grace. Abiding, not striving nor struggling; looking off unto Him; trusting Him for present power; trusting Him to subdue all inward corruption; resting in the love of an almighty Saviour, in the conscious joy of a complete salvation, a salvation 'from all sin' (this is His Word); willing that His will should truly be supreme—this is not new, and yet 'tis new to me. I feel as though the first dawning of a glorious day had risen upon me. I hail it with trembling, yet with trust. I seem to have got to the edge only, but of a sea which is boundless; to have sipped only, but of that which fully satisfies. Christ literally all seems to me now the power, the only power for service; the only ground for unchanging joy. May He lead us into the realization of His unfathomable fullness." (Edman)

It was as if a light came on in the life of this China missionary. He said latter of his experience with McCarthy's letter, "As I read, I saw it all. I looked to Jesus; and when I saw, oh how the joy flowed!" That day, his life and ministry changed. Secular history makes little note of Hudson Taylor. With God controlling his life, his achievements did not get the scribes attention. However, heaven's gates opened to a multitude of Chinese through his ministry. Writing to his sister of his new found life and ministry he said; "The Vine now I see, is not the root merely, but all—root, stem, branches, twigs, leaves, flowers, fruit: and Jesus is not only that: He is soil and sunshine, air and showers, and ten thousand times more than we have ever dreamed, wished for or needed." (Edman)

Oh, the joy of seeing this truth! Hudson Taylor was said to be the "object lesson of quietness." He drew from the "bank of heaven" every farthing of his daily income. He was a man that could hear God.

That is Victory

When you are forgotten, or neglected, or purposely set at naught, and you smile inwardly in the oversight, that is Victory.

When your good is evil spoken of, and your wishes are crossed, your taste offended, your advice disregarded, your opinion ridiculed, and you take it all in patient and loving silence..., that is Victory.

When you are content (as God's will for you) with any food, any raiment, any society, any solitude, any interruption..., that is Victory.

When you can bear with any disorder, any irregularity and unpunctuality, any annoyance..., that is Victory.

When you can stand face to face with waste, folly, extravagance, spiritual insensibility, and endure it all as Jesus endured it..., that is Victory.

When you never care to record your own good works, or to itch after commendation, when you can truly love to be unknown..., that is Victory.
—Unknown

Chapter Five

I Don't Want to Be a Missionary!

S ome years ago, I read a testimony of a young lady who was afraid of accepting Christ as her savior. Her reason was that if she ever gave her life to Christ, He would send her to the mission field. So, she resisted the Holy Spirit's drawing all through her teen years. Finally, in her early twenties and still rebelling against the Spirit of God, she attended a church during their evening service. At the end of the message, she found herself under such deep conviction she could no longer resist the Holy Spirit's call. She confessed her sins and sought the person of Christ with all of her heart. As a result she was born from above. Immediately, the call to the mission field overwhelmed her. She joyfully yielded her life at that instant to become a missionary.

What was the difference? The new indwelling Jesus Christ was the change. When He flooded her soul with His life, she totally responded to His life's calling upon her. At her salvation, God transformed her desires and completed *her* life and calling. Life without Christ is desolate, fruitless, and totally incomplete. Her call to missions came from the foundation of the world and it was *"without repentance."* It was with her all of her young years and she knew in her spirit that it was God's intention for her. Also during those years, satan had fought her call until the day she was bought by the blood of Calvary and brought into the Kingdom. God says, *"For the gifts and calling of God are without repentance"* (Romans 11:29). This verse in the Amplified states: *"For God's gifts and His call are irrevocable. He never withdraws them once they are given, and He does not change His mind about those to whom He gives His grace or to whom He sends His call"*.

Through the study of God's Word, I have come to the position of believing a person is not called to preach, but is born to preach—and this from the foundation of the world. In other words, God made the decision and chose them before time as we know it. As stated earlier, God saved me at the age of twenty-three, but even as a little child, I knew that someday I would be preaching the gospel. God's voice spoke continually to my spirit man.

Prior to my born again experience, I lived completely separated from the person of Jesus Christ. As a teenager and into my early twenties, God had no time or place in my life. I had no use for Him other than to use His name in vain. Still, way in the back of my mind, there was the constant thought that someday I would be a preacher.

Then one day, through a set of God-ordained circumstances, God answered the prayers of my Grandmother. God broke me. The Holy Spirit presented Jesus Christ to my heart in an overwhelming way. In His glorious presence, I repented of my sins and accepted His Son. At that instant, He saved me. At the same instant I was overwhelmed with the fact that I must preach the Gospel. I surrendered my life to Him that morning.

God has a perfect daily plan for every born again believer. It is called His will. My beloved, you will never know true joy until you have known the place of walking totally in the Spirit of Christ....in His kingdom come, in His will be done. That is where true life is—in Him. To receive this place in your Christian life means going after Jesus with all of your might. He must be sought after.

Such seeking results in the presentation that brings

transformation. It brings total change into your life. However, there can never be transformation until there has been presentation. Nothing will change until you are willing to give up everything you are. Please understand that I am not just talking about salvation; I am talking about selling out totally to God. Only at that point will you experience His personal will in your life.

Looking at John 5:44 we find: *"How can ye believe, which receive honor one of another, and seek not the honor that cometh from God only?"* In the Amplified version, this verse reads:

> **How is it possible for you to believe—how can you learn to believe—who (are content to seek for and) receive praise and honor and glory from one another, and do not seek the praise and honor and glory which come from Him who alone is God?**

Do not miss the meaning of this incredible verse. The question from God is: How is it possible to believe or learn to believe if you operate in religious pride? Satan's trap is self. As a baby is totally wrapped up in its own needs and wants, so is the baby Christian. "I want to be the center of all that is going on" is the cry from within. The enemy fans the carnal flames of fire that consume the average Christians of today. The *"envying, and strife, and divisions"* of I Corinthians 3:3 fill the disciples of self, whereas growing Christians experience growing faith.

> **For ye are yet carnal: for whereas [there is] among you envying, and strife, and divisions, are ye not carnal, and walk as men (I Corinthians 3:3)?**

It is imperative that you understand this in order to go on with God. You must not walk as a flesh Christian!

Repeating our earlier analogy, a baby first sits up, then one day stands until a confidence builds for the first step alone. Then it achieves more as boldness becomes the norm in its daily existence. All who are truly born again (God's way) and have the residing Holy Spirit within, believe the miracles of God. They do not question that all God speaks of in the Bible is not only true, but happened just as God stated.

The object is to transfer these truths from the Holy Spirit within us to our human spirit to the point they become experiential in living. You must attack and crucify pride until the abandoned soul-flesh becomes one with God's Spirit, and He becomes the One! From there, you will then believe by His faith (Galatians 2:20). We must believe by His faith for the Spirit teaches us here that all honor and glory go to and come from Him who alone is God.

> **For You are great and work wonders! You alone are God (Psalm 86:10 Amplified).**

Beloved, please do not forget what this chapter is all about. Our subject is bringing the Christian into the place of hearing from God within, as we have stated in many ways. I cannot repeat too often that making Christ the absolute center of our lives is the foundation of hearing from God within.

How Do I Get That?

Always remember that you must align what you hear in your spirit with the Word of God. The Word of God will never contradict what you hear from the Spirit of God. If there is a contradiction, then what you are hearing inside is not the Holy Spirit.

"Well," you say, "Brother Bonner, I want praise from God. I want to be His obedient child. What must be done to accomplish that?" In the father-son relationship in my family, I praise my son (who runs this ministry) when he accomplishes and excels in an area. I have discovered that when I do share with him my joy, there comes an even greater effort from him to achieve to his greatest abilities. Obedience to God always brings blessings. You can only realize this when you constantly pursue God's will. And, if you are a believer, will know when you are in the center of His will. His blessings overwhelm you. Oh, what joy to be one with Him and He to be the One!

Let me share once more what you will experience in obedience. When we seek to bring glory to the Father, He in return builds within us a desire to receive praise and glory from Him. The joy of that posture is so overwhelming we then make a constant effort to move toward Him. We do this in order to have our lives motivated into His personal will.

As a child, I wanted to please my father. However, he was so busy that he was hardly ever home. When he was, he seemed to have little time for me. There was nothing at that point I could do to get his attention. By the same position, we should desire with all of our hearts to please *"Abba"* (daddy), for our precious heavenly Father has all the time for us we desire.

> **For [the Spirit which] you have now received [is] not a spirit of slavery to put you once more in bondage to fear, but you have received the Spirit of adoption [the Spirit producing sonship] in [the bliss of] which we cry, Abba (Father)! (Romans 8:15 Amplified).**

He wants fellowship. He adores us beyond all comprehension. He awaits our prayer and praise. In return, He loves us with an undying love and is ready to give to us Himself in and through our lives. He will give us His complete attention. As the chorus says, "Oh, the glory of His presence."

With this in mind, look into your heart at this moment. What motivates you? Is it a desire to be recognized before your church? Is it perhaps to receive some position of authority such as a deacon or elder or teacher in order to be acknowledged for your good deeds or alms? What is your attitude when passed over and not praised? Are you totally and excitedly yielded to Jesus regardless of the assignment? You must understand that the totally committed, yielded–to–Christ Christian in today's church structure of religion stands alone. In fact, when you actively pursue the personal will of Jesus Christ through your life and He becomes your life, in this world you will be misunderstood.

A bit of prose that expresses this perfectly is entitled, *"That is Victory"*:

> When you are forgotten, or neglected, or purposely set at naught, and you smile inwardly in the oversight, that is Victory.
> When your good is evil spoken of, and your wishes are crossed, your taste offended, your advice disregarded, your opinion ridiculed, and you take it all

in patient and loving silence..., that is Victory.

When you are content (as God's will for you) with any food, any raiment, any society, any solitude, any interruption..., that is Victory.

When you can bear with any disorder, any irregularity and unpunctuality, any annoyance..., that is Victory.

When you can stand face to face with waste, folly, extravagance, spiritual insensibility, and endure it all as Jesus endured it..., that is Victory.

When you never care to record your own good works, or to itch after commendation, when you can truly love to be unknown..., that is Victory.

Unknown

Also, beloved, that is the mark of maturity.

To Be or Not To Be

As we have stated previously, the vast majority of all Christian religion of today has no room to allow the person of Christ to take His rightful place within. In that kind of setting, when a person comes along who really walks in a hearing position in the Spirit with their life of answered prayer; when they operate in a praise-peace position in the midst of all turmoil; when they have constant victory and joy over all circumstances, then religion says: "There is something wrong with that person! He's happy all the time! He is always studying the Bible. He wants to pray about everything." Some may even say, "You know, I feel so uncomfortable when I get around him."

How many times have I heard of those who walk with God making others uneasy in their presence! This response comes from the demonic strongholds in their lives. Darkness is always wary of light. When they come into the presence of someone who is truly walking with God, they will put a tag on their faith-walk by saying, "He has gone totally off the deep end! All he ever wants to talk about is Jesus. He won't be negative or critical. You can't talk to him about anyone. All he wants to do is pray. I don't like to be around him. He's too spiritual. He's not living in the real world." Well, for your information, he is. God intends for us to be filled with *"joy unspeakable and full of glory"* and to live with Him in the heavenlies while here on this earth.

Someone has well said that the Christian of today is so subnormal that when he encounters the presence of a normal Christian he thinks he is abnormal! Please understand that I am not trying to be negative at this point. What I am trying to share with you is simply this: When you present your life to Christ and you desire (totally) God's personal will, you will change completely. That is what being transformed means (Romans 12:2).

With this in mind, Deuteronomy 6:5 states, *"And thou shalt love the LORD thy God with all thine heart, and with all thy soul, and with all thy might."* Beloved, you will love the Lord that much when you give your life over totally to what God promises in Galatians 5:22-24. Jesus Christ is alive! You are living in Him if you choose to be "filled with" and "walk in" the Holy Spirit of God. If you do not, you will hear but not understand the language of God in your heart. This means being trampled on in the world's system as you sip your baby milk. It is time to grow up. It is your choice. As Shakespeare wrote, "To be or not to be, that is the question." I urge you "to be." Determine to be constantly filled with the Holy Spirit. *You must be in order to hear.*

Samuel Logan Brengle was a man whose life was changed dramatically by the filling of the Holy Spirit in the late nineteenth century. He was a preacher from Boston who found that he himself was his greatest hindrance to effective ministry. As he searched the Scripture, yearning for a fuller revelation of the living God, he found that he must empty himself before he could be filled with the Spirit. As he looked to Christ he discovered his own brokenness. He wrote:

> I saw the humility of Jesus, and my pride; the meekness of Jesus, and my temper; the lowliness of Jesus, and my ambition; the purity of Jesus, and my unclean heart; the faithfulness of Jesus, and the deceitfulness of my heart; the unselfishness of Jesus, and my selfishness; the trust and faith of Jesus, and my doubts and unbelief; the holiness of Jesus, and my unholiness. I got my eyes off everybody but Jesus and myself, and I came to loathe myself.

He desired to be a great preacher, thinking that a great

preacher would do more for the glory of God than a mediocre one. Finally, in utter desperation, he prayed. "Lord, I wanted to be an eloquent preacher, but if by stammering and stuttering I can bring greater glory to Thee than by eloquence, then let me stammer and stutter!"

The problem of pride was settled, yet there remained the matter of cleansing from sin. Though emptied of self and self-seeking, he was not filled with God and his heart was still hungry. He recorded what happened next in these words:

> For several weeks I had been searching the Scriptures, ransacking my heart, humbling my soul, and crying to God almost day and night for a pure heart and the baptism with the Holy Ghost, when one glad, sweet day this text suddenly opened to my understanding: *"If we confess our sins, He is faithful and just to forgive our sins, and to cleanse us from all unrighteousness"* (1 John 1:9); and I was enabled to believe without any doubt that the precious Blood cleansed my heart, even mine, from all sin. Shortly after that, while reading these words of Jesus to Martha: *"I am the resurrection and the life; he that believeth on Me, though he were dead, yet shall he live; and he that liveth and believeth on Me shall never die"* (John 11:26), instantly my heart was melted like wax before fire; Jesus Christ was revealed to my spiritual consciousness, revealed in me, and my soul was filled with unutterable love. I walked in a heaven of love. Then one day, with amazement, I said to a friend: "This is the perfect love about which the Apostle John wrote; but it is beyond all I dreamed of; in it is personality; this love thinks, wills, talks with me, corrects me, instructs and teaches me." And then I knew that God the Holy Ghost was in this love and this love was God, for God is love.
>
> Oh, the rapture mingled with reverential, holy fear for it is a rapturous, yet divinely fearful thing to be indwelt by the Holy Ghost, to be a temple of the Living God! Great heights are always opposite great depths, and from the heights of this blessed experience many have plunged into the dark depths of

fanaticism. But we must not draw back from the experience through fear. All danger will be avoided by meekness and lowliness of heart; by keeping an open, teachable spirit, in a word, by looking steadily unto Jesus, to whom the Holy Spirit continually points us: for He would not have us fix our attention exclusively upon Himself and His work in us, but also upon the Crucified One and His work for us, that we may walk in the steps of Him whose Blood purchases our pardon, and makes and keeps us clean. (Edman)

Samuel Logan Brengle chose to be filled with the Spirit. He could hear God's voice, and his life had a powerful impact on the Boston of his day. I pray that the same will be true of you wherever God places you.

There is a wonderful poem by Dr. A.B. Simpson that fits well here.

Himself

Once it was the blessing, now it is the Lord;
Once it was the feeling, now it is His Word;
Once His gifts I wanted, now the Giver own;
Once I sought for healing, now Himself alone.

Once 'twas painful trying, now 'tis perfect trust;
Once a half salvation, now the uttermost;
Once 'twas ceaseless holding, now He holds me fast;
Once 'twas constant drifting, now my anchor's cast.

Once 'twas busy planning now 'tis trustful prayer;
Once 'twas anxious caring, now He has the care;
Once 'twas what I wanted, now what Jesus says;
Once 'twas constant asking, now 'tis ceaseless praise.

Once it was my working, His it hence shall be;
Once I tried to use Him, now He uses me,
Once the power I wanted, now the Mighty One;
Once for self I labored, now for Him alone. (Edman)

Christ must be first in the life of the one who wants to come to a hearing place.

While a daily devotional hour is vital for saturating our minds with Christ, it is not enough. All during the day in the chinks of time between the things we find ourselves obliged to do, there are moments when our minds ask, "What's next?" In these chinks of time, ask Him: "Lord, think Thy thoughts in my mind. What is on Thy mind for me to do now?" When we ask Christ, "What's next?," we tune in and give Him a chance to pour His ideas through our enkindled imagination. If we persist, it becomes a habit. It takes some effort, but it is worth a million times what it costs. It is possible for everybody, everywhere. Even if we are surrounded by throngs of people we can continue to talk silently with our invisible friend. We need not close our eyes nor change our position nor move our lips. Thinking about Christ constantly is easy to understand. It is not easy to do.

— Frank Laubach

Chapter Six

A Whole New World

L et me share with you how I studied the Bible when I first received Christ at the age of 23. I knew nothing of God's Word other than the Lord's Prayer. When I began, through prayer the Lord led me to start in the book of Matthew. As I would read a verse, the Holy Spirit would then stop me to pray. My petition was always: "Lord, take this verse of Scripture and open my mind to its meaning." Without exception, as I meditated and sought Him for each verse, He spoke to me at the level of my spiritual walk at the time.

Please understand what I am saying here. Your faith life (revelation) expands as you grow in Christ, just as natural strength and intelligence grow in your physical body. For this reason alone, you must study the Bible constantly. Plain common sense says you would not strive to teach a small child the ABC's and calculus at the same time. His reasoning and retaining power has yet to develop. In the same manner, your understanding constantly expands as you grow in Christ. I have spent a lifetime of Bible study using this same method—never leaving a particular verse in question until God has revealed and quickened something to me. Many, many times I would have to read it over and over, going over prior verses, waiting until light came on its meaning.

Yes, I do use many of the available reference materials that I trust. They are invaluable. However, some of my greatest moments with God have been those times of Bible study during which He quickened and spoke to me intuitively. I do not want to sound like I have arrived at total biblical knowledge. You must understand, as of this writing, I have spent 42 years searching the Scriptures, but constantly I find wondrous, deeper truths in verses I have read many times before. It all has to do with where a person is in his spiritual growth level. The Bible is not a library of ancient information, but a "living mind" so infinite and so vast that, at man's greatest knowledge of the Word, he has only scratched the surface. There is a whole new world in there!

Through this method, I began to get a vital and working knowledge of God and His mind as revealed in Scripture. Through this method, I soon discovered that the Bible is a living book filled with life, and the breath of God's Holy Spirit moves upon it.

> **Every Scripture is Godbreathed (given by His inspiration) and profitable for instruction, for reproof and conviction of sin, for correction of error and discipline in obedience, [and] for training in righteousness (in holy living, in conformity to God's will in thought, purpose, and action) (II Timothy 3:16 Amplified).**

You must always be very careful to stay with the Word and not go by your feelings. A fine line separates divine revelation and human gnosticism (mystical wisdom and knowledge). God speaks through His Word and will quicken your heart, however, you must make sure you hear His voice. Again, never fail to test and cross reference with Scripture what you hear intuitively. If it does not correspond, then you have encountered a false spirit of Jesus.

But [now] I am fearful, lest that even as the serpent beguiled Eve by his cunning, so your minds may be corrupted and seduced from wholehearted and sincere and pure devotion to Christ. For [you seem readily to endure it] if a man comes and preaches another Jesus than the One we preached, or if you receive a different spirit from the [Spirit] you [once] received or a different gospel from the one you [then] received and welcomed; you tolerate [all that] well enough! Yet I consider myself as in no way inferior to these [precious] extra-super [false] apostles (II Corinthians 11:3-5 Amplified).

No matter what you feel or experience, test everything by the living Word of God.

I was 23 years of age when I was born again. Within six weeks, I entered the military service. One of the first things I received there was a Gideon New Testament. I still have it after 42 years. I recall reading it constantly in those first weeks of basic training. At night, I would sleep with it in my hand. I had been very deep into the world. I knew nothing of how to pray. In those first weeks of basic training, when the command of "lights out" came, instead of lying in my bunk and praying, I would wait until all were asleep and go to a window. There I would get on my knees, look straight up at the stars and talk to God. I thought that was the way people were supposed to pray. No one told me that God was in me, though I knew something inside had radically changed. As I look back now, I know God placed me in that environment to get my complete attention. The military was my first step to obedience and brokenness.

Wholly Means Holy as Holy Means Wholly

In those days of sheer simplicity, my major emphasis in prayer was telling God I loved Him. How many times did I thank Him for saving me? He responded by quickening my spirit with His. I truly knew that He loved me. Oh, how I was captured by this wondrous presence! Those were wonderful beginning days in Christ for I was shut up to His Word. As strange as it may sound to those who have experienced it, I enjoyed the discipline of basic training in the military. I am saying this to express that the greatest joy I have ever known in my life has always come at times when I pursued Jesus Christ with all of my heart. Again, the result of all of this was the beginning of my transformation that came only at my presentation. To know God's will and mind, you must present yourself constantly to Christ—a living sacrifice.

In this present leisure-oriented society, the word "instant" has become a marketing phenomenon. The world has geared itself to play. Whole complexes are built for entertainment. In this mobile existence, personal relationships become temporary.

But thou, O Daniel, shut up the words, and seal the book, [even] to the time of the end: many shall run to and fro, and knowledge shall be increased (Daniel 12:4).

People make no lasting commitments of any kind. Marriage today is passé. "Don't get tied down." How true is God's Word when He describes in Matthew 24 the world system in this final period of history!

That this lifestyle has moved into God's kingdom is even more heartbreaking. The church is no longer the center of family life. The church has become a center for activities rather than a place of worship: a place to play and not to pray. It now has almost no effect on society. Lawyers are now being trained in how to sue the church and to tap into its wealth. Church buildings are being burned as those who have been raised through two generations without God respond in hatred against the restrictions God places on His children in the Bible. What we are experiencing now is only the beginning if revival does not come. Man's inner being is totally alienated from God's voice. There is no conviction. "If it feels good, do it," the system says.

Regardless of these events, God still speaks to His children. We find one of the key Scriptures of the Bible explaining how He communicates to the listening mind in the Old Testament. I have, for a Christian lifetime, leaned upon this Scripture as truth and made it work through my life. You can find it in Proverbs 16:3 in the Amplified Bible.

Roll your works upon the Lord—commit and trust them wholly to Him; [He will cause your thoughts to become agreeable to His will, and] so shall your plans be established and succeed.

Probably the key to all ongoing biblical revelation and direction for daily living is in this wonderful verse. To hear from God you must choose to press yourself into His presence. You make a choice of will. You must go after Him. Serving Him means getting out of the business of dead religion and into hearing (in your spirit man) by revelation. You accomplish this by rolling *"your works upon the Lord ..."* The Word means exactly what it says. In this case, you are to put all of your trust or load on Him.

In the historic time of Proverbs, as well as for many centuries to follow, people carried loads on their back held by two straps over the shoulders. When transferring the load to another, they would place one arm through the strap standing to one side of the person. The individual with the load would then stand straight and roll the burden onto the back of the other person who would bend to receive it. They would then exchange the strap from the other arm and that person would slip his arm through. The rolling procedure not only exchanged the load, but the second person received it in a balanced fashion and could carry the weight on his shoulders.

This is what God is saying here. For us to receive His mind and will we must transfer (transform) our life to His. We must commit and trust everything wholly to Him. As you can see, religious works have no place here. When we abandon, transfer, and seek Him with all of our heart, we give everything over to Him completely. He then balances and carries our load, and we carry only the load of His will. As we learned earlier from Romans 12:1, this is our *"reasonable service."*

We must position ourselves by *"delight"* in His presence

so we may come to this place with Him. This comes only by our complete desire for oneness with the Holy Spirit.

> **For it is through Him that we both [whether far off or near] now have an introduction (access) by one [Holy] Spirit to the Father [so that we are able to approach Him] (Ephesians 2:18 Amplified).**

This also means that we no longer want to serve in our own works of the flesh (religion), but we crave only to serve Christ. He becomes our life. This is the process God accomplishes in us as we commit and trust our lives wholly to Him. Furthermore, God will only use you from this place — or better said — use Himself through you. Stated another way, the Scripture says, *"Christ in you, the hope of Glory."*

The first step in the procedure for hearing from God is you must roll your works (your life) upon Christ. In this process, you commit and trust all to Him completely. Having moved yourself then into hearing distance, you are ready for the next step God promises in His unchanging Word. He pledges to you that if you will *"roll your works,"* or as we stated previously, *"present your body a living sacrifice, holy, acceptable,"* He will begin the process of conforming you to His standard.

God only uses a person according to His own standard. That standard is never their religious works. We are to "be holy as He is holy." Therefore, our own holiness is not the measure. The true standard of righteousness He demands is the level of His holiness within us. This is a profound truth. As we have stated several times, holiness is not an experience but a person. That person is Jesus Christ living in you. You are only as holy as you have submitted to Christ's control of your life and permitted His life to flow through you. So, in Proverbs 16:3, "wholly" means holy, whereas in Romans 12:1, holy means "wholly."

Go With the Flow

From this position of complete submission to God at the current level of your growth, He then states He will *"cause your thoughts to become agreeable with His will"* (Proverbs 16:3 Amplified). There it is. I have people tell me all the time, "I do not hear from God," or "God never speaks to me about anything." What they are saying indicates one of several problems:

First, they could be lost. The voice of the Holy Spirit in a lost person's life speaks only for conviction, repentance, and salvation. His ministry is to draw them to new birth for *"no man cometh to the Father except the Spirit draw him."*

Second, if you are a baby Christian, you cannot discern or understand the voice of God. He deals with the immature in chastisement and the maturing in "truth." He deals with them only from the level of where they are as a child of God: whether infant or adolescent. The voice of God still speaks to all who make it their desire to understand.

Finally, as we continue growing up in Christ, we then long to be with Him in a constant relationship. The more we are around Him (our choice), the more we grow and learn of Him and His perfect will and life through us. This is what this portion of Scripture means when it says, *"He will cause your thoughts to become agreeable with His will"* (Proverbs 16:3, Amplified). The rolling of works is our part. The speaking to our mind is His. Those who do not hear never "present" or "roll."

As we put these teachings into practice, our minds become one with His (transformed). Then, in growth, as we study Scripture, we suddenly "know" a truth as living instead of written only. It quickens and overwhelms our soul with the Gospel (something that is true, Webster's Dictionary). During these processes, the Spirit brings us to a greater faith in Christ and His Word. Truth pierces through to the *"inward parts,"* even to the point of *"dividing asunder."*

For the Word that God speaks is alive and full of power [making it active, operative, energizing, and effective]; it is sharper than any two-edged sword, penetrating to the dividing line of the breath of life (soul) and [the immortal] spirit, and of joints and marrow [of the deepest parts of our nature], exposing and sifting and analyzing and judging the very thoughts and purposes of the heart (Hebrews 4:12 Amplified).

From that position and through the study of the Word, coupled with constant prayer, you will begin to know what to do in every situation. You will learn how to respond to all things in a godly manner. In your life, His kingdom has come; His will is being done through you *"as it is in heaven."* He will speak intuitively to your mind in all matters.

From this place in your Christian growth, one of God's choice verses on hearing becomes reality. He says, *"Let this mind be in you that is in Christ Jesus"* (Philippians 2:5). By the same token, as you have rolled your works onto Him, you will find that *"your thoughts will become agreeable to His will"* (Proverbs 16:3, Amplified). These are His thoughts given to you. What an incredible place to be in life! You are right in the center of His mind and will, with Him continuing His work on this earth through you. All the time you know from that place He will constantly *"guide you into all truth."* He will conduct the circumstances of your life. As the song says, "What glory, honor, and power"; the total joy of His continuing His work through you! It is an incredible place to be. If you want to know the feelings of one who experienced this joyous place, it is stated in Philippians 3:10...

[For my determined purpose is] that I may know Him [that I may progressively become more deeply and intimately acquainted with Him, perceiving and recognizing and understanding the wonders of His Person more strongly and more clearly], and that I may in that same way come to know the power outflowing from His resurrection [which it exerts over believers], and that I may so share His sufferings as to be continually transformed [in spirit into His likeness even] to His death, [in the hope] (Amplified).

Finally, the Amplified version of Proverbs 16:3 states, *"...so shall your plans be established and succeed."* Again, how many times in 40 years of ministry have I tried to answer the question, "Brother Bonner, how do you hear from God?" It all has to do with position. If you are standing away from Him (religion), then you must be told what to do (law). However, if you are standing in Him (filled with the Spirit), then the voice of God operates from within and through you (grace). From this place you are filled and covered with Him. You then go with the flow or the direction of the Spirit. Therein God conducts His business through your life according to His will and plan. This continuing process is the servant's (slave's) life. Oh, what joy it is to be crucified with Christ, and live in resurrection and power (Galatians 2:20).

Getting the perfect equipment (Jesus)

Jesus Christ is the ultimate example in Scripture of a person who could hear the voice of God and respond in obedience. We must remember that He was not only the Son of God but also the Son of Man. As the perfect Son of Man, He had to hear God's voice in the inner man as we must also do today. As a result He was a man of answered prayer. He understood complete submission and the yielding of His life to the Spirit of God. In John 5:19 and 30, Jesus explained His total dependence on the Father.

> **So Jesus answered them by saying, I assure you, most solemnly I tell you, the Son is able to do nothing of Himself (of His own accord); but He is able to do only what He sees the Father doing, for whatever the Father does is what the Son does in the same way [in His turn] (John 5:19 Amplified).**

> **I am able to do nothing from Myself [independently, of My own accord-but only as I am taught by God and as I get His orders]. Even as I hear, I judge [I decide as I am bidden to decide. As the voice comes to Me, so I give a decision], and My judgment is right (just, righteous), because I do not seek or consult My own will [I have no desire to do what is pleasing to Myself, My own aim, My own purpose] but only the will and pleasure of the Father Who sent Me (John 5:30 Amplified).**

He saw what the Father was doing, received His orders, was taught by God and could hear God's voice. His only desire was to please the Father Who sent Him. The following excerpt from my Brokenness book sheds light on how this develops in the believer.

In John 5:17, 19, and 30, Jesus declares of Himself, *"I can of mine own self do nothing."* All of the profound occurrences as Jesus walked upon this earth, were the manifestations of the glory and power of God through the Son, in answer to the prayers of Jesus. Christ constantly *"went apart to pray."* Oh beloved, grace through prayer, extends from us into the lives of others the miracle of God's power and His glory. We, however, must be broken as was Jesus. To be able to hear some day as we stand before him, *"Well done, thou good and faithful servant,"* is the greatest reward of heaven. To have that happen, we must be as contrite as Jesus when He wept before the Father in agonizing prayer. The Word gives an account of His brokenness in Hebrews 5:7-9. Not only did He pray specific prayers from the mind of the Father, but *"His supplications were with strong crying and tears."* Jesus constantly wept for us while praying before God.

In the Amplified, Hebrew 5:7 reads, *"He was heard because of His reverence toward God."* Beloved please understand that the word "reverence" means to be "submitted," "dedicated," "yielded," "worshipful," and totally given over to God, and that in desperation you beg to be used of Him. Then, as we've said time and again, to be useful for God, we must abandon ourselves to Him, knowing that we have no righteousness within ourselves, for it is all as *"filthy rags."* From that position in our transformed righteousness, it suddenly becomes His life, for we're only as righteous as He is righteous in us. The level of brokenness in our lives is determined by our yieldedness to Him and to His consuming control over all that we are. In the case of the Scripture we just read, the words *"His reverence"* simply mean *"Godly fear and piety."* Jesus abstained from anything that would bring separation between the Father and Him. So must we be in Him.

Now, the Spirit was with Him. Incidentally, it is the same Spirit which indwells those of us who are born again. Many times, however, we discover that as we're about to enter into an event we become desperately uneasy inside, knowing that something is wrong. That uneasiness is the Holy Spirit speaking to your spirit in an effort to give you direction in a matter. The Scripture says that the Holy Spirit will guide us into all truth (John 16:13). Jesus was so pure in His walk in the Spirit that He was never hindered by evil. He faced the sins that we face and stood totally against them. Such was His position with God, and so pure was His heart toward the Father. Hebrews 5:7 in the Amplified concludes, *"He shrank from the horrors of separation from the bright presence of the Father."*

Then, Hebrews 5:8 says it all. *"Although He was a son, He learned [active, special] obedience through what He suffered,"* (Amplified). He left heaven. He came to earth virgin-born. He lived a life without sin, died on the cross, and rose from the grave. He destroyed all the power of the enemy through those events. He was God in the flesh. But it must be understood that Jesus was the Son of Man as well as the Son of God. As a human, He learned suffering. So must we learn obedience through suffering.

Oh, my beloved, do not run from your tribulation. Submit sovereignly to God in praise in the midst of your trials. Become joyfully excited as you transfer your spirit to His, allowing Him to consume you by taking those burdens from you as you *"cast all your care upon Him"* (I Peter 5:7). So walk through your sorrows in righteousness, excitement, and joy, with *"the peace of God that passeth understanding"* (Philippians 4:7). Then you bear testimony to those around you of the sovereignty of a holy God and His presence in your life. Oh, for the privilege of being

His! It can happen to all born-again believers who will fight their flesh and force themselves constantly toward Christ with all their hearts, (Romans 12:1-2).

Pray to be broken. Hebrews 5:9 states of Jesus:

His completed experience made Him perfect [in equipment]. He became the Author and Source of eternal salvation to all those who give heed and obey Him (Amplified).

Now, that may not mean much to you at this point, but, my beloved, someday when you get home, having passed through this flesh either by death or by rapture, and you stand in the midst of God's presence, you will be overwhelmed by the knowledge in your spirit in its glorified state of what Christ has performed for you. You will then fall at His feet crying, "Glory, worthy, worthy is the Lamb." You will praise Him! You will exalt Him! you will glorify His name! It will be the spontaneous breaking of a well-spring within you. Oh, the joy you will experience at that point of sudden pure knowledge of who He is and what He has done. It is so far beyond all that you can conceive that it takes the sublimed mind to understand. You will then realize that He learned His obedience through what He suffered, and you will praise Him in pure adoration. What a price He paid for us! Now, before we can move from this glorious truth of the breaking of Christ for His ministry, we must realize that we are in co-identification with Him when we are broken, for only through this experience does He minister by way of His life. In the book of Isaiah, We are given the message of how God prepared Christ for His purpose and our redemption.

In Chapter 53, we have the will of God through the mind of the prophet to give to us the description of what really happened to our Christ. Verse 2 begins by telling us about Jesus early years. "As a tender plant and a root out of dry ground did He grow up." The Bible then says that there was "no beauty in Him," describing His physical features. God gave us a physical description of His Son. Jesus was a normal, every day, run of the mill, Jewish man. He was not strong, masculine, tall, commanding of appearance, or of great authority. He had not even a powerful voice that would startle a listener and claim his attention. God gave Him no beauty that any one would desire his flesh or His personality. You see, the ministry of Christ was to allow the Father to perform through Him so that by the work of the Father in Him, the world would know that Jesus was the Messiah. . . .

Now, remember that in order to experience Christ's life through us, we must enter into the same realm in which he walked to bring forth His ministry. For it is through brokenness that we are birthed into the dimension of the victorious Christian life. To live from *"glory to glory,"* we must go from breaking to breaking. At the end of each experience of brokenness is a new measure of the quality of Christ through our lives, and a deeper level of faith in which to believe Him. Awaiting, on the other side of tribulation is the ministry that has been written out for us in heaven, according to Ephesians 2:10. That ministry becomes, *"Thy kingdom come, thy will be done, on earth as it is in heaven."* We focus our entire attention and life upon Christ. Through us, He begins to develop the character of His will. From there, we move into a higher dimension of yieldedness to Him, growing in the attributes of His life, which are *"love, joy, peace,"* and all the rest of Galatians 5:22-24.

To walk like Christ walked and to live like Christ lived, our minds must be filled with Christ. God says in Psalm 91:14-15; (Amplified):

Because he has set his love upon Me, therefore will I deliver him; I will set him on high, because he knows and understands My name [has a personal knowledge of my mercy, love, and kindness—trusts and relies on Me,

**knowing I will never forsake him, no, never].
He shall call upon Me, and I will answer him;
I will be with him in trouble, I will deliver him
and honor him.**

Here we find that if we will set our love upon God, He will deliver us. He promises that if we call upon Him, He will answer. What a wondrous place to be. Totally conformed in His will and He directing us from within. Frank Laubach writes:

> While a daily devotional hour is vital for saturating our minds with Christ, it is not enough. All during the day in the chinks of time between the things we find ourselves obliged to do, there are moments when our minds ask, "What's next?" In these chinks of time, ask Him: "Lord, think Thy thoughts in my mind. What is on Thy mind for me to do now?" When we ask Christ, "What's next?," we tune in and give Him a chance to pour His ideas through our enkindled imagination. If we persist, it becomes a habit. It takes some effort, but it is worth a million times what it costs. It is possible for everybody, everywhere. Even if we are surrounded by throngs of people we can continue to talk silently with our invisible friend. We need not close our eyes nor change our position nor move our lips. Thinking about Christ constantly is easy to understand. It is not easy to do. Yet there is a way to do it without stopping our other occupations. It is to acquire a new way of thinking. Thinking is a process of talking to your inner self. Instead of talking to yourself talk to the invisible Christ.

He Is Sleeping

God gives us another wonderful example of this in Hebrews 11 which states they all received the "report." That is, by God's revelation, they knew before it happened, and believed it to happen, and it did. How many times in Scripture do we find this declared!

Elijah stood on the mount having challenged those who

were in control of the nation to a duel to find out if Baal be god or Jehovah be God. As the prophets of Baal, prophets of the Lake assembled, they prepared their altars to bring fire down from heaven to prove their god Baal to be the only true god. Under the taunting of Elijah, when several hours had gone by and they could not arouse Baal's attention, they began to display a more radical form of chanting by cutting themselves in blood sacrifice. After they had exhausted themselves and perhaps some had even died, Elijah cried out over the noise of their pleading, "Perhaps he is sleeping."

Finally, when it was evident that Baal's satanic powers of fear and witchcraft did not operate in the presence of a true man of God, the people turned to the prophet Elijah and waited in wonder. Could it be that they were falsely led and Jehovah is the one true God? To prepare for the evidence of this reality, Elijah had the ruined altar of God rebuilt. With wood and sacrifice placed in order, he had a trench dug around the waiting mound. He sent men three times to Cherith's brook to fill four barrels of water and pour them over the sacrifice. Finally, he turned his voice toward God and cried, *"Lord God of Abraham, Isaac and Israel, let it be known this day that thou art God in Israel and that I am thy servant, and that I have done all these things at Thy Word."* Upon his prayer, God rained fire down and *"consumed the burnt sacrifice, and the wood, and the stones, and the dust, and licked up the water that was in the trench"* (I Kings 18:38). God did it all with indelible finality.

The Lord, as always, proved Himself to be God. In fact, He will have the last word in all earthly history. To those who denied His Son's redeeming work on the cross, that word will be "depart." The result of their departure will be, *"and in hell they lift up their eyes"* (Luke 16:25).

Now, getting back to Elijah, look at this whole scenario. Did he just sit around and think up this whole event? Was he bored and looking for something to do that afternoon in an effort to kill time? Certainly not. The Spirit of God spoke to him the whole plan. He knew this was to be done. With it he also knew beforehand the total outcome. His part was to hear and then obey the will of God. As he did, Israel saw again the complete sovereignty of Holy God,

Jehovah. He first received a word and then his faith became substance.

We find also this same process demonstrated when Moses heard and then obeyed. As a result the Israelites were delivered from Egypt. Paul also heard and obeyed. Most of all, Jesus heard and obeyed. In fact, as we have seen, the key to His earthly ministry was hearing.

> **I can of mine own self do nothing: as I hear, I judge: and my judgment is just; because I seek not mine own will, but the will of the Father which hath sent me (John 5:30).**

Thank God for His obedience and our eternal salvation.

Beloved, how many times have I known in my spirit what I had to do and, before beginning the process, I knew the outcome? How wondrous that experience. God speaks to the heart. He will direct your steps. As you obey, He will continue the ministry of Christ through you.

George Mueller was one of the greatest men of prayer in the nineteenth century. He wrote, "I live in the spirit of prayer. I pray as I walk, when I lie down, and when I arise. The answers are always coming. Thousands and ten thousands of times have my prayers been answered. When once I am persuaded a thing is right, I go on praying for it until the answer comes." George Mueller heard in his heart the voice of God.

God accomplishes this by His speaking to your mind. Upon receiving a Word from Him, you act as if it is done. This becomes the "agreement with His own plan." As the ultimate outcome, His will is done *"on earth as it is in heaven."*

God works His wonderful will through yielding and obedient human vessels. His *"eyes are searching"* for such vessels *"to show Himself strong through"* (II Chronicles 16:9 Amplified). Another verse that speaks to this issue is Ezekiel 22:30 Amplified.

> **And I sought for a man among them who should build up the wall and stand in the gap before Me for the land, that I should not destroy it; but I found none.**

Another way to say it: First, you know His will; then, you

supply the faith. The result is that He does the work through you. John Calvin stated: "God will do nothing on earth except in answer to believing prayer."

When you "roll" everything upon God and give up your life completely, He covers your mind with His. You have also brought yourself to the place of Philippians 2:5 which states: *"Let this mind be in you, which was also in Christ Jesus."*

Prayer, Deep Prayer, Real Prayer

When Mary Warburton Booth went to India, she was excited about her opportunity for ministry there. However, after five years of labor with no fruit, she became discouraged. She returned home with thoughts of quitting the work. She attended a Keswick Convention, and there God restirred her call within. Armed with a new vision and brokenness she returned. She changed one procedure from her prior ministry. She put prayer first in every endeavor. God's Glory fell on her work. She later wrote a poem that revealed her inner experience of Christ's control of her life:

> God called me out to work for Him
>   And Oh, what joy and love
> Came to my life as I went forth
>   To win for heaven above.
> As time went on I saw the need,
>   Gross darkness everywhere.
> So in the forefront of my work
>   I supplemented prayer.
> God kept me on to work for Him,
>   And day by day I learned
> How sacred was my blessed task
>   As o'er the lost I yearned.
> With will and purpose on I toiled,
>   Oft' questioning - What availed
> This weary striving day by day?
>   In winning souls I failed.
> He kept me on, and on I went,
>   And then there came a day
> When all was changed - I put it down

That you might know the way -
He stopped me in my self-planned toil,
  And laid my purpose bare,
And I ashamed, rebuked, went down
  In agonizing prayer.
He heard me as I turned to Him,
  And He just turned to me,
Took both my hands in His, and said,
  "Great victories you shall see.
The secret is for you to know
  That what you do and where,
The fundamental work for you
  Is prayer, deep prayer, real prayer."
And oh, the victories He has wrought
  And oh, the souls He won,
When I have prayed right through to God
  He brought them one by one.
Until I look and am amazed
  For prayer has brought release:
And now I pray, whatever else
  "Lord keep me on my knees."

Mary Warburton Booth learned to roll her works upon the Lord.

Another of God's great giants of prayer was William Bramwell. He wrote "I am all weakness, indeed, I see nothing will do but a continual dependence, and a living upon His mercy—and oh the depth of mercy. It is continual prayer that brings the soul into all the glory. . . . I am striving in continual prayer to live nearer to God than I have ever done; and He brings my soul into closer union. I live with Jesus; He is my all. Oh He lays me at His feet! I am less than nothing in His sight." It is evident that William Bramwell was acquainted with God's wondrous Holy Spirit. He was in a hearing place.

Religion or Righteousness?

Ephesians 6 illustrates this powerful position. There Paul describes how God dresses us in His whole armor when we seek Him fully. Each piece is the person of Christ Himself. As the Christian grows, the Holy Spirit adds each unit—corresponding with his continued maturing. Then, as a final act of growing in faith, He places on the believer the helmet of salvation. This is actually His mind over ours. Through His eyes we then see the Word of God as a sword of offense, not defense. From that revelation, according to the next verse, He places us in the battlefield. Always the battlefield is prayer. He declares, *"Praying always with all prayer and supplication in the Spirit"* (Ephesians 6:18). With the mind of Christ and the sword of the Spirit we enter into battle with the enemy. In this conflict, Christ always wins. He does it through believers who can hear and agree.

Transformation begins only after daily presentation and growth. The antithesis of this is one saying: "Why can't I find the will of God for my life?" What he is really saying is: "I am not yet yielded fully to the Lord Jesus Christ. I am not committed or pursuing Him. He speaks to me in words of more than one syllable and I don't understand yet."

We have seen repeatedly that to find His path or will, you must desire Jesus with all your being. You must desire this to the point that you would be willing to lay anything down, take up anything, just to make Jesus actively Lord. You can easily see why so few Christians come to this life. It takes work and complete commitment. It must be your life's goal.

To establish this relationship with Him, you begin by praying, "Whatever it takes to break me, do it. I will be crucified with Christ." Then in praise tell Him: "I give You my total life; I commit everything that I am to You." This will begin His work in you. Then, as the process of breaking and growth comes, He becomes more to you than all past unforgiveness and roots of bitterness. You will begin to lose your hatred and besetting sins. This is the process as He becomes one with you in your spirit. From this emerges His revealed will for your life.

Herein, in essence, is the message of Romans 12:1-2, as well as Proverbs 16:3. First comes presentation; second, transformation; and, third comes that which we desire most—His revelation (P/T=GW). The reverse of this: no revelation means there is no presentation and, consequently, no transformation. It is up to you. Will it be religion or righteousness, flesh or faith, manipulation or manifestation?

Only you can give the answer.

I must give you one important admonition again. As we have stated several times, you must be careful to test the voice you hear. Satan is a counterfeiter. He can seduce baby Christians into believing they are hearing God's voice. If you believe you are listening to God and you are filled with anger, bitterness or even religion, check what you are hearing with the Word of God. If it does not line up with Scripture, don't do it. Again, the Word is the plumbline of God's will. He will never depart from it. His statement is to "study to show yourself approved ..." It is one thing to know about Jesus. It is another to *"know Him"* (II Timothy 2:15).

The Palest Ink

A classic illustration of "hearing" comes from the life of Martin Luther, the man that God used to begin the Reformation. Walter Trobisch, who wrote a booklet on a forty page letter Luther sent to his barber, tells this story. The barber had asked a simple question of his famous customer, "How do you pray?" When Luther completed his response, he published it in 1585 under the title *A Simple Way to Pray, For a Good Friend*. It stands as a Christian classic that establishes in writing how he waited upon God for His mind. Some excerpts will help to verify what we have stated in this chapter. Luther writes:

> I believe in God, the Father Almighty, Creator of heaven and earth. First of all, if you allow it to happen, a great light shines here in your heart. This light teaches you in a few words something which could never be expressed in all languages, nor described in many books, namely: What you are, where you are, where you come from, where heaven and earth come from.
>
> It often happens that I lose myself in such rich thoughts [literally, that my thoughts go for a walk] in one petition of the Lord's Prayer, and then I let all other six petitions go. When such rich, good thoughts come, one should let the other prayers go

and give room to these thoughts. Listen to them in silence and by no means suppress them. For here the Holy Spirit Himself is preaching, and one word of His sermon is better than thousands of our own prayers. Therefore, I have often learned more in one prayer than I could have obtained from much reading and thinking.

Here Luther is not only speaking to God, but hearing as well. This is the most important aspect of prayer, for God answers no prayers but His own. We must be able to hear from God and respond in His will. The key to all praying is *hearing*. If you cannot "hear," you cannot agree with God, which is the imperative.

Martin Luther understood the position of hearing "in the spirit man." He goes on to say to his barber: "I report to you again what I said when I talked to you about the Lord's Prayer. If the Holy Spirit should come when these thoughts are in your mind and begins to preach to your heart, giving you rich and enlightened thoughts, then give Him the honor. Let your pre-conceived ideas go. Be quiet and listen to Him who can talk better than you can. Note what He proclaims and write it down so you will experience miracles. As David says: *'Open my eyes that I may behold wondrous things out of thy law'*" (Psalm 119:18).

How well Luther states the position of "hearing," for God does speak to the inner man. As you study, meditate upon the Word. As you pray, listen to the still small voice, always establishing what you hear in the Word of God for proof and virtue. God will speak to your mind.

In writing this booklet (published by Inter-Varsity Press), Walter Trobisch makes a profound statement in closing. He urges us to always have pen and pad close by as we pray. The reason is God speaks to our mind and we loose it. He quotes here a Chinese proverb that says, "The palest ink is stronger than the strongest memory." Learn to listen, and deal seriously with what you hear.

You Know That You Know

Now, you say, "Brother Bonner, how can I find what

God is personally doing through my life? How can I hear from God?" Revelation simply means the ability to hear and discern what the Holy Spirit says to you. What then is discernment? It is an inner perception of that which is God's personal will or plan and thereby, in faith, acting upon it. It also means that you are absolutely sure of having received God's will in a matter; so much so that you launch out by faith, knowing full well God's power is working through you. You know that you know it is God. You also know that you have received God's mandate in your spirit and can begin to believe it with your heart in order that you can see it with your eyes.

Discernment, stated another way, means to have an inner knowing as shown here in the Word:

> **But as for you, (the sacred appointment, the unction) the anointing which you received from Him, abides (permanently) in you; (so) then you have no need that any one should instruct you. But just as His anointing teaches you concerning everything, and is true, and is no falsehood, so you must abide—live, never to depart (rooted to Him, knit to Him) just as (His anointing) has taught you (to do). And now, little children, abide (live, remain permanently) in Him, so that when He is made visible, we may have and enjoy perfect confidence (boldness, assurance) and not be ashamed and shrink from Him at His coming. If you know (perceive and are sure) that He (Christ) is absolutely righteous (conforming to the Father's will in purpose, thought and action), you may also know (be sure) that every one who does righteously (and is therefore in like manner conformed to the divine will) is born (begotten) of Him (God) (1 John 2: 27-29 Amplified).**

This Scripture tells us God's power and direction will come if we will abide in Him. God states: *"His anointing teaches you concerning everything."* To have this happen in your life, you must abide and grow in Him. This is your active part. You are commanded to constantly pursue Jesus. You have to go after Him with all of your mind, soul, and body. You must constantly keep Christ first. Your priority in life must be Jesus Christ so that the Father controls your life and flows through it. These same verses from the King James translation state:

> **But the anointing which ye have received of him abideth in you, and ye need not that any man teach you: but as the same anointing teacheth you of all things, and is truth, and is no lie, and even as it hath taught you, ye shall abide in him. And now, little children, abide in him; that, when he shall appear, we may have confidence, and not be ashamed before him at his coming. If ye know that he is righteous, ye know that every one that doeth righteousness is born of him (1 John 2:27-29).**

"Righteousness" means right standing with God, or standing right where God is in you. Therefore, when you walk in the Spirit the activity of the Spirit is evident in your life. The indelible sign you are born again is that you show the activity of Christ to and through you. However, if you rebel against His will, God then breaks you in order to bring you back into His mind (Hebrews 12:3-15). God does this with all of His children who give up the struggle for holiness and yield to their carnal desires.

> **Now the works of the flesh are manifest, which are [these]; Adultery, fornication, uncleanness, lasciviousness, Idolatry, witch-craft, hatred, variance, emulations, wrath, strife, seditions, heresies, Envyings, murders, drunkenness, revellings, and such like: of the which I tell you before, as I have also told [you] in time past, that they which do such things shall not inherit the kingdom of God (Galatians 5:19-21).**

I urge you to do whatever is necessary to bring yourself into the will of God and stay in it. Go after Him with all of your heart. Walk in His light.

Incidentally, when you talk to others about walking in God's will, the subject becomes so overwhelming and complex that many Christians have no understanding of what you mean. Yet, it is simply God acting out His pre-arranged plan to and through their lives. Satan tries to make this all complex and confusing, but it is not. Christ has a purpose and a plan for all who have received Him. Based on your obedience, you can get into line with what God desires to happen in your life.

> **For we are his workmanship, created in Christ Jesus unto good works, which God hath before ordained that we should walk in them (Ephesians 2:10).**

Never forget that the individual who does the greatest damage to satan's work is the committed believer who walks in the Spirit. His life is startlingly simple, but profoundly powerful. He remains filled with joy in the midst of adversity, with love in the presence of anger, with beauty when attacked by ashes. He is an enigma to all human carnal attitudes and personalities. He cannot be controlled by demonic force for he is walking in the Spirit, acting in the Spirit and living day by day in the Spirit. Most of all, He is doing the work of the Spirit. What joy unspeakable. Praise the Lord, it can happen to any who obey and *"seek....first the kingdom of God"* (Matthew 6:33).

Begin now to confess your sins; forgive all who have hurt you. Then pursue Christ, present your body to Him, and live abundantly. In so doing, you will encounter the position of knowing and experiencing God's will for your life. In loosing your life, you will find it. It is incredible. In fact, it is life in true abundance. Why not choose now to "roll your works" upon the Lord? Why not lose your life so you can find His?

Be still sometimes - so still that
God may speak,
And make His voice heard in thy
waiting heart.
Sometimes the hush of His calm
presence seek;
From all the world's confusion
come apart,
And silence even praise, and
breathe no prayer,
But only wait for Him to meet thee
there.
Be still sometimes! Be still enough
to hear
The faintest whisper of His voice,
and feel
The touch of His dear hand, when
He draws near,
Himself unto thy spirit to reveal.
God will His deepest truths to thee
make known
Only when thou art silent and
alone.

— Edith H. Divall

Chapter Seven

"My Sheep Hear My Voice"

Many people become confused when you talk about being able to hear from God in your spirit. They ask: "Is there actually a voice that speaks to you within?" As stated earlier, God speaks intuitively to the mind. Intuitive means "prompted by natural instinct" (Webster). We may describe it better as: "knowing within that a thing is true."

Another way to describe it is the old saying about women's intuition. My mother used this very formidably in my young life. Somehow she always knew. I could not get away with a thing. I believe now that a lot of this had to do with the look on my face.

Now, the capacity for hearing from God begins at the point of salvation in the life of the believer. A miracle happens when the Holy Spirit enters into the spirit of man. He brings into the Christian the language of God. He also brings with Him the pre-planned ministry God wants to perform through that person's life.

We find this doctrine in John 16:7 and 12-15, as well as Ephesians 2:10. Look at Jesus' words in John 16:7, 12-15, in the Amplified Bible:

> **However, I am telling you nothing but the truth when I say, it is profitable—good, expedient, advantageous—for you that I go away. Because if I do not go away, the Comforter [counselor, helper, advocate, intercessor, strengthener, standby] will not come to you—into close fellowship with you. But if I go away, I will send him to you—to be in close fellowship with you. I have still many things to say to you, but you are not able to bear them, nor to take them upon you, nor to grasp them now. But when He, the Spirit of Truth [the truth-giving Spirit] comes, He will guide you into all the truth—the whole, full truth. For He will not speak His own message—of His own authority—but He will tell whatever He hears [from the Father, He will give the message that has been given to Him] and He will announce and declare to you the things that are to come—that will happen in the future. He will honor and glorify Me, because He will take of [receive, draw upon] what is mine and will reveal [declare, disclose, transmit] it to you. Everything that the Father has is mine. That is what I meant when I said that He will take the things that are mine and will reveal [declare, disclose, transmit] them to you.**

From these Scriptures, we see the position of the interworking (in today's computer world language, the "networking") of the Holy Spirit within us. His Spirit couples with ours in a living position. We are then one with Christ. In these verses, we find that He directs our steps and ministers through us according to His personal will. The Bible not only calls the Holy Spirit our counselor, but also helper, advocate, intercessor, strengthener, and standby. In the light of this, we will deal in this chapter with the true ministry of intercession and what it means to hear from God within.

From the depths of these verses, the Spirit reveals to us the truth of what God wants us to understand about this matter. At salvation, the Holy Spirit comes within us to begin performing the plan that God has for us. In His first work, He conforms us to the image of Christ from the inside out. From there, as we obey Him, He produces the ministry of Christ through us on the outside. He does this either by prayer or by performing His sovereign will in our lives. Remember also that real prayer is not the position of the body, but is the condition of the heart to hear and obey.

The Bible commands us to *"walk in the Spirit."* It also exhorts us to be *"led of the Spirit."* It further commands us to be *"filled with the Spirit,"* which simply means the seeking-yielding of our life to Him until we overflow with the Spirit.

> **And do not get drunk with wine, for that is debauchery; but ever be filled and stimulated with the [Holy] Spirit (Ephesians 5:18 Amplified).**

From there, He uses our life and operates through us the glory of the power of His resurrection.

> **We were buried therefore with Him by the baptism into death, so that just as Christ was raised from the dead by the glorious [power] of the Father, so we too might [habitually] live and behave in newness of life (Romans 6:4 Amplified).**

The Holy Spirit's working within us is also the performance of God through us. This happens only at the level of our willingness to allow Him to do what He desires to do. How many times and how many ways have I said this in this writing? You must understand that we are directed by *"the hidden man of the heart."*

One of the verses I constantly pray for my own personal life is Philippians 3:10...

> **[For my determined purpose is] that I may know Him [that I may progressively become**

more deeply and intimately acquainted with Him, perceiving and recognizing and understanding the wonders of His Person more strongly and more clearly], and that I may in that same way come to know the power outflowing from His resurrection [which it exerts over believers], and that I may so share His sufferings as to be continually transformed [in spirit into His likeness even] to His death (Philippians 3:10 Amplified).

To minister the glory of the power of the cross takes a constant pursuing of our lives toward Christ. It is like getting dressed and going to school every day. We press our life toward Him in prayer, in Bible study, in the activity of subduing the flesh by not being critical or negative. We also praise Him through the wonderful times of adversity.

Consider it wholly joyful, my brethren, whenever you are enveloped in or encounter trials of any sort or fall into various temptations. Be assured and understand that the trial and proving of your faith bring out endurance and steadfastness and patience (James 1:2-3 Amplified).

By this experience, we are enlarged. At the same time, we allow the person of Christ within us to be sufficient in every need.

Answer Me when I call, O God of my righteousness (uprightness, justice, and right standing with You)! You have freed me when I was hemmed in and enlarged me when I was in distress; have mercy upon me and hear my prayer (Psalm 4:1 Amplified).

His grace is truly sufficient for us.

Turn Your Radio On

We spoke earlier of an old Gospel hymn, "Turn Your Radio On." I am old enough to remember when radio was the major source of in-home entertainment. I can recall as a child having favorite programs I would never miss. One was a daily, Monday through Friday, broadcast that came on at 5:30. The name of that program was *Jack Armstrong, The All-American Boy*. I desired to do all the things that he did. Oh, to live the adventures that he experienced. However, to do so, I would have to—or so the sponsor implied—eat a cereal called "Wheaties".

Another program I would never miss was *The Green Hornet.* The hero had a formidable Asian sidekick by the name of "Kato," who was his constant companion and karate expert extraordinare. Together, they could do anything. Oh, how I longed for their abilities in my life. Again, the sponsor implied my first step to this kind of greatness was that I had to drink a formula to give me strength, and power, and super human abilities. It was called "Ovaltine." Then, still vivid in my memory, is another daily 30-minute episode that I would "glue" myself to the radio to catch. It began with the hardy sounds of a masked man crying, "High-O Silver, Away". He was none other than the Lone Ranger. He also had a sidekick who was constantly at his side, his faithful Indian companion, Tonto. As I recall, he could do everything.

Believing their great abilities were tied directly to their diet, I remember eating what the sponsor wanted me to eat. However, as I recall, I never had the experiences they did. Perhaps it was because I did not have a sidekick to help me out. Needless to say, my breakfasts always held great expectation! Not in their content (I did not like Ovaltine), but in the hoped for results—but alas ...

Then, as the evening hours came, there were other favorite programs during the week: *Jack Benny and his faithful friend, Rochester.* Then there was *Fibber McGee and Molly,* always with the expected-unexpected when someone would open a familiar closet door. We knew from past broadcasts that there would be things crashing to the floor as Molly admonished the person, "Don't touch that door!" It was good for front-room hysteria. You always knew that sometime in the broadcast it was coming.

Beloved, for me to enjoy these broadcasts, there were things I had to do to get my favorite radio shows. Number one, I had to be there at the right day and hour. Number two, I had to have my radio in good working order, plugged in, and tuned to the right frequency to receive the broadcast. This is the point. Suppose you have a radio. With it you have the electrical outlet that will produce the power within the set to receive the signal. You have it plugged into the wall. You turn the radio on. You turn up the volume to where you can hear it, and you sit down to listen. But nothing comes out of the speaker. You wait expectantly for the familiar introduction that includes the music and background sound effects that tell you your wait is over. Still nothing. What is lacking? You must have the mental ability to turn the dial and tune the set to the frequency where it can receive the signal. You must tune in to the right channel.

Herein lies the greatest problem in the lives of many believers. The power is there. When you are born again, the Holy Spirit comes to live within. You receive all the Holy Spirit you are ever going to get at that moment. Now begins the process of the Holy Spirit getting all of you. However, for it to happen, you must tune your life into His frequency so you are able to hear.

Paul describes this in Philippians 3:10. He states, *"That I may know Him, and the power of His resurrection, and the fellowship of His sufferings, being made conformable unto His death."* All that the Christian will ever need is wrapped up in this declaration: First, to know Him means to become one with Christ. Second, resurrection power means to operate in His power and will. Third, to enter the fellowship of His sufferings means to be constantly changed through brokenness to a deeper walk and relationship with Him.

Meditation Means Transformation

Because of busy schedules and an "instant" mind set, we have become a people who allow others to think for us. Many times, our spiritual experience is tied up with a personality or a religious structure. For instance, we decide where to worship because, "I like that preacher," or "That was my mother's denomination, so we will go there." Because of busy travel, family and work schedules, there is no time for the study of God's Word, so we become trapped in tradition. Our doctrine and personal Bible study habits become predicated on the depth of the Sunday morning message and the pastor's dedication to truth. Then, if we really feel the need to "study deeper," we may tune our radio or television to some "trusted" teacher of like mind and faith.

Such a Christian life produces no growth and no exercising of faith. The Scriptures are the written Word of God. You are setting aside the person of Jesus when you do not *"study to show yourself approved."* Reading and meditating on God's Word is another form of prayer. You search the Scriptures and He then begins to speak through your inner man. As with the minds of little children, His voice will begin to have more meaning, and then increased understanding will come.

The beginning of Wisdom is: get Wisdom (skillful and godly Wisdom)! [For skillful and godly Wisdom is the principal thing.] And with all you have gotten, get understanding (discernment, comprehension, and interpretation) (Proverbs 4:7 Amplified).

Learning or Living

Several years ago, we took a family to Israel with us to begin mission work there. After they entered language school in Jerusalem, it took them months to begin to understand the Hebrew language. After several years, they became proficient enough to begin ministering to the nationals.

In the meantime, their two children had entered public school. In the process of playing with other children, plus picking up words from their teachers, they were conversant in the language in just a few months. It was amusing when the parents who were studying the language formally had to go to their children, ages seven and nine, to get help on certain words. To the parents, it was a learning position. To the children, it was a living position. Their "classroom" was being a part of the daily lives of other children.

Such is meditation. When you turn to Scripture in a living, searching way, God will speak to you. When you meditate on a verse, the person of Christ (the Holy Spirit) expands your spiritual mind so you can understand.

> **In the beginning [before all time] was the Word (Christ), and the Word was with God, and the Word was God Himself. He was present originally with God (John 1:1-2 Amplified).**

According to Webster's definition, "meditate" means, "to consider or examine attentively or deliberately." God will not give you *"stone for bread"* when you seek Him in a matter. Meditation means to stay your mind on Him until He opens your heart to understanding.

God promises in Joshua 1:8:

> **"This book of law shall not depart out of your mouth, but you shall meditate on it day and night, that you may observe and do according to all that is written in it; for then you shall make your way prosperous, and then you shall deal wisely and have good success" (Amplified).**

When you meditate (stay your mind) on a verse, not only will He open that verse, but He will transfer you into its reality. The Scripture is filled with admonitions to meditate. It is the schoolroom of His will.

> **But his delight and desire are in the law of the Lord, and on His law (the precepts, the instructions, the teachings of God) he habitually meditates (ponders and studies) by day and by night (Psalm 1:2 Amplified).**

> **When I remember You upon my bed and**

meditate on You in the night watches (Psalm 63:6 Amplified).

Take time to study Psalms 119. All through this lengthy chapter God constantly emphasizes meditation. Then, in Isaiah 33:18 and in I Timothy 4:15, God directs us to believe.

Your mind will meditate on the terror: [asking] Where is he who counted? Where is he who weighed the tribute? Where is he who counted the towers (Isaiah 33:18 Amplified)?

Practice and cultivate and meditate upon these duties; throw yourself wholly into them [as your ministry], so that your progress may be evident to everybody (I Timothy 4:15 Amplified).

The Miracles of Meditation

In the course of meditation, comes God's transformation, or the renewing of the mind. One of the great examples of this is the story of a Catholic monk who lived in Florence, Italy from 1487 to his martyrdom in 1498. His name was Savonarola. Through this man's life, revival broke out in that city.

Upon arrival to the region, he became broken over the corruption, vice, and immorality that had grown from the roots of the Catholic Church. In the early days of his life, he would carry a burden for and weep for the sins of the people there. He carried the weight of the conditions he saw propagated by the leaders of the church. History said he would lie on his face for hours in a contrite state for the church. He would weep and pray as he sought God's intervention. He sought God in everything and in the process experienced transformation.

When Savonarola was 22, he wrote a thesis titled *Contempt of the World*. In this writing, he compared his day with the sins of Sodom and Gomorra.

Finally, in a much-broken state, he entered a monastery.

He purposed to fast and pray for the needs of those around him. His total time went into the study of the Word, coupled with fasting and prayer. His mind became one with Christ's and he began to hear the voice of God within his spirit. By that voice, Savonarola began his public ministry. Totally submerged in the Holy Spirit, and one with Christ through meditation on His Word, he spoke with the voice of God. Without fear or partiality, he exposed the sins of the people.

As always, with this presence of power through a person committed to Christ, revival broke out among the people, who cried aloud in repentance before God. History states conviction through the power of the Holy Spirit so gripped them that they were half dazed and speechless.

This man was so in union with the Holy Spirit that, as he attended the services, his face would outwardly glow with God's presence. He would stay in that state for up to five hours, lost in the presence of God's glory. Then in his broken state he would speak the Word of God, not from hearsay, but with power. The fires of revival swept the area for eight years. The crowds would wait hours just to hear from God through him. God did mighty works through this yielded vessel. He prophesied with the mind of God. He stopped armies by standing between them and the city. He taught the people how to establish a democratic government.

The morality of the area changed as God's Spirit melted the hearts of all who were there. God so moved the people that they destroyed anything that might influence them away from His will. They burned books as well as other worldly idols. One writer also states, "a great octagonal pyramid of worldly objects was created in the public square in Florence; it towered in seven stages, 60 feet high and 240 feet in circumference. While bells tolled, the people sang hymns and the fire burned, reminiscent of Paul's revival bonfire in Ephesus"

Many also of those who were now believers came making full confession and thoroughly exposing their [former deceptive and evil] practices. And many of those who had

practiced curious, magical arts collected their books and [throwing them, book after book, on the pile] burned them in the sight of everybody. When they counted the value of them, they found it amounted to 50,000 pieces of silver (about $9,300). Thus the Word of the Lord [concerning the attainment through Christ of eternal salvation in the kingdom of God] grew and spread and intensified, prevailing mightily (Acts 19:18-20 Amplified).

All of this had not gone unnoticed as this man's rebellion against the Catholic Church of his day angered a corrupt pope, along with his cardinals and priests. Just as religion dealt death to Jesus, so they saw death as the only way to stop this man of God. They tortured him to get him to recant his stand. They bound him by ropes. They tied his hands behind him, raised him high off the floor and then released him. Just before impact, the rope went taut, tearing at his body and pulling apart his joints and muscles. They placed burning coals on the bottom of his feet trying to persuade him to deny his stand.

His only answer was to beg God for forgiveness for those who were persecuting him. His final words to the mob sent by the church to destroy him were, "Should I not die willingly for Him who suffered so much for me?" According to the record, at that moment, he yielded himself so much to God that he seemed totally separate from the events that followed. As Christ was hanged upon a cross in the name of religion, so was Savonarola hanged by the neck and then his body burned (Duewell). Oh, the joyous response in heaven when he came home! Although he made many mistakes he was totally ambitious for God alone.

We can very simply state the key to his life and ministry in one word: meditation. When you meditate upon God's Word with a desire to hear, not merely seeking to (make the Bible agree with you), the Holy Spirit will begin to conform you to the image of Christ from the inside out. From there, God will begin to reconcile you to His image and transform you by the renewing of your mind (Romans 12:1-2). Savonarola sought God with all of his being and found Him.

Again, this is the miracle of meditation. This is finding and hearing the mind of Christ.

Jesus states in John 16:33, *"These things I have spoken unto you, that in me ye might have peace. In the world ye shall have tribulation: but be of good cheer; I have overcome the world."* God the Father says in Job 37:14 *"Stand still and consider the wondrous works of God."* Also in Psalm 46:10 He declares *"Be still and know that I am God: I will be exalted among the heathen, I will be exalted in the earth."* A poem by Edith H. Divall expresses well the importance of meditation.

> Be still sometimes - so still that God may speak,
> And make His voice heard in thy waiting heart.
> Sometimes the hush of His calm presence seek;
> From all the world's confusion come apart,
> And silence even praise, and breathe no prayer,
> But only wait for Him to meet thee there.
> Be still sometimes! Be still enough to hear
> The faintest whisper of His voice, and feel
> The touch of His dear hand, when He draws near,
> Himself unto thy spirit to reveal.
> God will His deepest truths to thee make known
> Only when thou art silent and alone.

We must take our lives and bring them back to God by force as previously stated. We must *"hunger and thirst," "seek," "knock," "strain," "pursue," "chase," "assault with violence,"* and *"labor to enter into the rest."* We must become what we already are: *"crucified," "reckoned dead to sin,"* and our bodies presented as living sacrifices. All of this brings us to the transformation, the metamorphosis, the changing from our life to His. Much of this takes place when we are silent and alone before the Lord. These processes tune you into God's mind and will. This brings daily growth. Lambs follow the flock; sheep hear His voice and follow the Shepherd. Lambs survive by milk; sheep eat from the green pastures to which the Shepherd leads them.

Herein is the ministry and the work of the Holy Spirit to bring you to a place of hearing God in your spirit. God does speak to our spirit intuitively. He impresses us. He directs us. He also speaks to us through the Word and quickens us as we study and meditate on Scripture. In doing so, He helps our infirmities, our flaws, and our physical, mental, and moral weaknesses. He creates and builds within us the character of Christ, building us up in Holy faith.

—Mickey Bonner

Chapter Eight

Abandon to God

Philippians 3:10–11 gives us the most enlightening declaration concerning the truth of brokenness before the Lord. The difference between life and death is spirit. If the spirit of a man is gone from his body, he is physically dead. If the Holy Spirit does not operate in the Christian's body, then he is spiritually dead in the sense that he is carnal and operates in the flesh.There is no fruit or supernatural living.

The best place to study this truth is in Romans, Chapters 6, 7, and 8. Do it slowly, painstakingly, and prayerfully; digging, begging, and seeking wisdom and revelation from every verse as you read it. These chapters are the x–rays which reveal where you really are and what is going on in your life.

Philippians 3:10 in the Amplified Bible lays a foundation for hearing from God. It says:

> ... [for my determined purpose is] that I may
> know Him—that I may progressively become
> more deeply and intimately acquainted with

Him, perceiving and recognizing and understanding [the wonders of His person] more strongly and clearly. And that I may in that same way come to know the power outflowing from His Resurrection [which it exerts over believers]; and that I may so share His sufferings as to be continually transformed [in spirit into His likeness even] to His death.

Then, verse 11 says:

. . . that if possible I may obtain to the [spiritual and moral] resurrection [that lifts me] out from among the dead [even while in the body].

The expression *"to know Him"* is a marriage phrase referring to the way a husband and wife become one. At this writing, my bride, Margaret, has been at my side for 42 years: through ministry, through raising a family, through hurts, and through blessings. As stated earlier, we have so become one that I know what she feels.

We have become, as the Scripture states, *"one flesh"* (Genesis 2:24). God has truly blessed me by selecting this girl for me, and by causing us to walk together as one. When I married her I did not go back to my parents' home that afternoon. We have stayed together these many years. In the process of our marriage, my knowledge of her did not come instantly. In fact, when I think that I have just about gotten a handle on who and what she is, she makes a left turn. She ends up going in a completely different direction. This is very unnerving to me because I like to see the end at the beginning. When I think I have her all figured out, something changes. Therefore, I must stay close; and, believe me, I do. I do this because I love her desperately and thank God for her life.

Now, suppose something happened in the world's system to stop all forms of transportation. It would not matter where I am in the world, I would somehow, some way, find my way back to her. To be with Margaret is to be home, whether it be at our ministry in the Philippines, Europe,

Africa, or our home in Texas.

In Philippians, Paul states essentially the same thing to us. Look at it once more:

> **[For my determined purpose is] that I may know Him [that I may progressively become more deeply and intimately acquainted with Him, perceiving and recognizing and understanding the wonders of His Person more strongly and more clearly], and that I may in that same way come to know the power outflowing from His resurrection [which it exerts over believers], and that I may so share His sufferings as to be continually transformed [in spirit into His likeness even] to His death, [in the hope] That if possible I may attain to the [spiritual and moral] resurrection [that lifts me] out from among the dead [even while in the body] (Philippians 3:10-11 Amplified).**

Beloved, I understand it. In my desire to belong to God totally, I want to serve Him with all that I am. How many times have I begged to be broken before the Lord! I must be His. Yet, after 42 years of Christianity, and 40 years of ministry in one form or another, I could never begin to touch where Paul was at that moment in his life.

Here he begs to become progressively and more deeply acquainted with Christ. Paul lived in a state of total abandonment to the Lord. At the time he wrote these divinely-inspired words his abode was a cold, dark prison. His fellowship is with a guard in the physical, and with the Holy Spirit in the spiritual. To some, the surroundings would be miserable; but Paul lived in a wonderful world of his own. He had come to the place of complete, transformed, sublime submission to God. He could truly give thanks for everything.

In that place, God's grace had become so sufficient that he fills this epistle with a symphony, a harmony, an all-consuming joy as he shares the oneness of Christ in his life. In the experience of giving himself over to his Lord, he has found firsthand knowledge of the wonders of His "Person." Now, he cries for more and more of Jesus. With

this abandonment comes the influence of Christ's resurrection and power. Vincent's wonderful translation of this
verse states it well, *"...the power it exerts over believers."*
The word *"exert"* means to bring to bear, especially with
sustained effort or lasting effect. How true this is of the
Spirit of God for Christ's power begins from the inside.

Through submission the believer moves to the filling of
the Spirit, which overflows and covers the outside. God
does this through prayer and the power of His consuming
presence in the life of the individual. Through this process,
come the mind of Christ, the ministry of Christ, and the
manifestation of Christ through the believer.

With it also comes all that Galatians 5:22-24 describes in
and through the life covered with the Spirit. This Scripture
explains the nature of that individual:

> **In contrast, the fruit of the Spirit is love,
> joy, peace, patience, kindness, generosity,
> faithfulness, gentleness, self-control. Against
> such there is no law. Now those who belong to
> Christ [Jesus] have crucified their flesh with
> its passions and desires (Amplified).**

The Christian who has yielded to this place suddenly finds
himself experiencing discernment. With it comes direction.
With that comes declaration of the power and the glory of
God through us in prayer.

Individuals who enter into school seeking to learn how
to communicate, how to read, how to respond, and how to
relate, through prescribed studies, begin to grow into a
maturing relationship with life. Suddenly, the direction for
their future begins to come into focus. Some feel directed to
the work of their hands. Others feel leading into the activity of their minds. So, a design begins to take place. Their
studies in high school begin to point to higher education.
Some move into engineering, some into teaching, or some
perhaps move into the medical arts. They align their academic training toward their goals. They finally graduate and
begin fulfilling their dreams, desires and, many times, their
divine calling.

Such was Paul in Philippians 3:11 that his one major

goal above all others was that he could attain to a present moral and spiritual resurrection. This would then lift him out of the world's system into a journey down the path of righteousness *"for His Name's sake."*

Listen again to Paul in Philippians 2:1-2, as he begins to open his heart to the place of *"right standing with God:"*

If there be therefore any consolation in Christ, if any comfort of love, if any fellowship of the spirit, if any bounds and mercies. Fulfill ye my joy, that ye be like minded, having the same love, being of one accord, of one mind.

The key phrase in these two verses is the line that states *"fellowship of the spirit."* Now, the word *"fellowship"* is the Greek word *"koinonia."* That word means to be on intimate terms with God.

Remember earlier, in John 16:7 in the Amplified Bible, the translation says of the Holy Spirit who lives with us that *"He is the comforter [counselor, helper, advocate, intercessor, strengthener, standby]."* Now, all of the ministries spoken of here are in us if the Holy Spirit possesses us and we desire to do what God designs to perform in our lives according to His will. What good is a counselor if we cannot speak to him? What good is a helper if he cannot reach us? What good is an advocate, a defense attorney, who cannot defend us? What good is an intercessor who hears from God but cannot agree with us in prayer? What good is a strengthener if he cannot respond to fortify us? What good is a standby who is not ready within our lives when our strength is gone? In this state, we are incapable of seeking help due to our own baby-like condition. We do not understand. The Holy Spirit is ready to extend God through us, but we do not know how to communicate with Him.

W. E. Vine explains *"koinonia"* this way in his *Expository Dictionary*: "A having in common, partnership, fellowship recognized and enjoyed, a participation in what is derived from the Holy Spirit." When we are one with Christ, we become one with each other. Those who see us then describe our relationship as, *"We love one another"* (I John 4:11).

Twice the Husband

God has given to our family a beautiful, new grandson, named Trey. Trey, is my son Mick and his wife Becky's first child. He loves his father and mother. Trey is beginning to talk at this writing. However, his communication is based on single words. His father works in our ministry. When his work is over and he goes home, I delight to see young Trey react to his dad's voice. When he hears his dad coming in, everything stops. He ceases whatever he is doing and turns to that voice. Not only does he smile, but he waits, anticipating being picked up and played with. This relationship between Trey and his dad gives us great light on how incredibly simple our faith ought to be. We should be just like a little child holding up its arms to the father, crying Abba (Daddy), desiring to be cared for, loved, spoken to, and directed. Oh, the comfort and security of being in God's arms! Oh, how He wants to direct our steps, if we would just reach for Him.

A marriage where one partner does not communicate with the other is a life in a prison of isolation. He goes his way and she goes hers. He has worked to pay the bills. She has spent a lifetime raising children and driving the family bus. Now the kids are gone. There is nothing to do. They find they are faced with each other on a daily basis. They have nothing to talk about; no common interests. Then one day there is retirement. As someone has well said, that word means "half the income, twice the husband." Soon satan moves in to divide. Bitterness becomes the watchword and hatred becomes the mediator of all communication. Then, except for occasional angry yelling, there comes silence. The marriage is all but dead. Love is gone. They cannot stand each other. How destitute that kind of relationship!

"Koinonia" means fellowship, the love of being together. In this desire for fellowship, God will answer if you speak to Him.

Call to Me and I will answer you and show you great and mighty things, fenced in and hidden, which you do not know (do not distinguish and recognize, have knowledge of and understand) (Jeremiah 33:3 Amplified).

Perhaps you will not understand His language at first. My grandson is learning single words like yes, no, light, nose, tree, and puppy—especially puppy. This stirs great excitement in our family when we hear him. In the same manner our communication with God comes first in the simplicity of one word at a time. First, we respond to voice inflection. We may not understand the word "no" in the language of the spirit. However, if we do not respond to it we will later experience the results of our misunderstanding.

Love is a language all its own. My grandson does not understand the word "love," but he understands my picking him up and holding him very close. He lays his head on my shoulder and puts his arms around my neck. My beloved friend, to me that is worth it all. He understands, when in strange surroundings or amidst loud noises that are unfamiliar to him, that for security he can reach for his mother or father, or for me or his grandmother. We hold him. Then he observes those noises and learns they will not hurt him as long as he is in the protective arms of love. When this assurance comes, he wants down immediately and he is off again. Such is our joyous love relationship with the Father.

Do you see it? Prayer is talking to God. Answered prayer is hearing from God and sensing the Holy Spirit in your life as He directs you. You begin by understanding the "yeses" and "nos" by the inflection of His Voice. Then you begin to operate in the principle "when in doubt, don't" as the Holy Spirit directs your path. Then one day, as you grow, you will learn a word, then words, then a sentence, and then a paragraph. Finally you begin to understand God's language. God communes, instructs, and directs you through the Word or through prayer. As you become His sheep, you will understand and obey His voice. You will joyously follow once you have experienced the wondrous joy of obedience. It is not a lifestyle to learn, but a life to live. It is a relationship of love.

Voice of God

The Scripture tells us much regarding the voice of God to the spirit of man. His voice not only gives direction for the believer's life, but also reveals the Lord's ministry through him. Tragically the activity of the vast majority of all Christians is the pursuit of man's plan to serve God. They hear their own voice, or the voice of a demon rather than their Lord's. In regard to God speaking to the Christian, Paul writes in Romans 8:26-27:

Likewise the Spirit also helpeth our infirmities; for we know not what we should pray for as we ought; but the Spirit itself maketh intercession for us with groanings which cannot be uttered. And He that searcheth the hearts, knoweth what is the mind of the Spirit because He maketh intercession for the saints according to the will of God.

Here God is speaking through the Apostle one of the deepest doctrines of prayer in the Word. It is called intercession. Again, all true prayer is the ministry of God's Spirit either to or through the believer. The imperative for all Christian experience is for the believer to find the mind of God. Without it, we stumble in the dark, playing religious games and never have an effective life or lifestyle in the Kingdom's work. From that position, satan is free to destroy those whom he pleases. No one is stopping him through prayer.

God says in verse 26 that we are infirm. The word "infirm" is an adjective which means "lacking physical, mental, or moral strength." For the most part people who have infirmities are incapable of operating at full capacity. They are limited. If their infirmities are physical, their activities are hindered in the physical realm. If their infirmities are mental, then they have an incapacity to cope with a structured life on a daily basis. I have visited Hong Kong many times. There I have encountered the Chinese language. I can hear it, but I cannot comprehend what they are saying. This is a form of infirmity. The vast majority of Christians have this same infirmity with the voice of God. It is there, but they cannot understand it.

Go With the Flow

One of the hardest things I have ever had to accept is my

own mother's bout with Alzheimer's. She died at 94 years of age. Just before she died, when I visited her, she remembered me but asked if I was married and had children. My heart was deeply grieved over this because she has been such a vital part of my family over the years. Her loving response has always been a blessing to our children. She was in an assisted living situation, and her equilibrium had so diminished they had to help her in everything she did. Her infirmities, both mental and physical, had consumed her life. It has been very hard for me to watch.

God says, as believers, we also have infirmities. One of these is we do not know what to pray for as we ought. The average Christian of today does not realize this. Called upon, they will take off in myriad directions in prayer. I have always felt the best way to tell where a person is with Christ is to listen to him pray. Sometimes I will meet with a pastor before a service and we will pray together. As a rule of thumb, the people you are going to minister to walk at the exact level of the pastor's prayer life. This will especially be the norm if he has been there several years. If he is a man of God and deeply broken before the Lord, the presence of the Holy Spirit shows in his life and voice. He prays from a conditioned, broken heart.

By the same standard you can tell if a pastor is a hireling. This is an individual who is moving his way through to a better opportunity (larger, more wealthy congregation), seeking greater results that expose his abilities as a church builder. You will find this kind of person praying *at* God. His praying will be speaking to the listener and not to the Lord. He usually speaks in well–refined diction that extols his mental capacities. God says they think they are heard for their much speaking and vain repetitions.

And when you pray, do not heap up phrases (multiply words, repeating the same ones over and over) as the Gentiles do, for they think they will be heard for their much speaking (Matthew 6:7 Amplified).

It is true that our spirits commune and that you can actually sense a relationship with God in the life of another believer. I can often walk into a church and listen to the music and tell you if it is performance-oriented or if it is worship-centered. I can usually tell if the congregation is without conviction (no prayer life). Believers with discernment can sense it atmospherically. Then when I stand to preach, if the church is a "flesh" church, I feel as I minister like I am running in water up to my neck. There is no liberty, no presence of the Holy Spirit. However, if the church is alive and prayer–based, and people are broken before God, it becomes a soaring experience. The presence of the Spirit of God is so wondrous that there is liberty. In that setting, a minister will end up preaching God's will. How wonderful it is to go with the Spirit's flow!

Such is the message of Romans 8. When we have battled ourselves into a believing relationship, the Spirit Himself begins to speak to our spirit. He gives us direction, correction, and finally, perfection for, at this stage, He is constantly perfecting us. Here we experience the changing into His image by living *"from glory to glory."* Suddenly, our ministries are His. His presence has captured our prayer and the Holy Spirit begins to minister the work of God through us. The individual who conducts a truth-seeking study of Romans, coupled with a desire to hear with a spiritual ear, will ultimately be brought spiritually through Chapters 6, 7, and 8 to this place of hearing. This is the meaning of Romans 8:26 and 27.

So too the [Holy] Spirit comes to our aid and bears us up in our weakness; for we do not know what prayer to offer nor how to offer it worthily as we ought, but the Spirit Himself goes to meet our supplication and pleads in our behalf with unspeakable yearnings and groanings too deep for utterance And He Who searches the hearts of men knows what is in the mind of the [Holy] Spirit [what His intent is], because the Spirit intercedes and pleads [before God] in behalf of the saints according to and in harmony with God's will (Amplified).

When we are in Christ Jesus and *"walk not after the flesh, but after the Spirit"* as the first verse of Romans 8 says, we become free. As the Holy Spirit begins to live the life of Christ through us, we experience the righteousness of the law. If we do not seek this walk and continue to operate in our religious activities, then the sixth verse of Romans 8 says we are carnally minded and filled with death. In fact, that sixth verse is a great test of your relationship with God. If you are carnally minded, you are negative and critical, caustic and bitter, filled with fear, and constantly looking for bad in everything. However, if you are broken, filled, and walking in God's Spirit, then no matter what happens to you, you are filled with Christ's life. You have peace, victory and excitement; and, most of all, you experience the *"joy unspeakable and full of glory."*

Romans 8 and Your Spiritual State

This is why it is so imperative for you to pray to be filled with the Holy Spirit. At that moment, you give over to God's Spirit and He begins to conduct, through you, the life of Christ. When that happens, He begins to set you free from besetting sin and the strongholds in your life.

We find this spiritual progression beginning in verse two of Romans 8. God cancels the penalty of death in that same verse. From there, He fulfills righteousness as we spoke of in verses 4 and 5. Then, He indwells the believer, the born-again Christian, with the life of Christ (verses 9 through 11). In the process, He gives life by ministering through the believer (in verse 10), and then He quickens the mortal body in verse 11. The Greek term here is *"zoopoieo,"* which means to make alive or be raised from the dead. Such is the glory of the filling of the Holy Spirit in the believer. From there, He mortifies the sinful members of our flesh. It is through the power of the Spirit that we reject these sins, deny them, and crucify the things that try to consume us (verse 13). Verse 14 records the result of all this process: the inward ministry of Christ begins to lead the child of God. With it comes the continued growth that brings adoption into His family in verse 15. Continuing on in growth, He then bears witness to and through us of our sonship and our relationship in verse 16.

When we have become what we are in Him, He then helps us in our infirmities (not knowing God's will) by telling us by His Spirit that for which we are to pray. It is the beginning of understanding *"Thy kingdom come, Thy will be done."* All of this is the process of growth as we *"grow in grace and knowledge."*

Herein is the ministry and the work of the Holy Spirit to bring you to a place of hearing God in your spirit. God does speak to our spirit intuitively. He impresses us. He directs us. He also speaks to us through the Word and quickens us as we study and meditate on Scripture. In doing so, He helps our infirmities, our flaws, and our physical, mental, and moral weaknesses. He creates and builds within us the character of Christ, building us up in Holy faith. He must do this in us because "God's ways are not our ways." He therefore speaks to us regarding His ways. *"We know not what to pray for as we ought,"* but the Holy Spirit within us makes intercessions (or, in essence, tells us) with groanings those things that cannot be uttered.

Many have written much about intercession over the years. It is an incredible ministry and yet it remains a mystery to multitudes. The word itself is from the Greek word *"huperentunchano,"* which means to "apply one's self to intercede for another." As stated earlier, the greatest example of intercession for all time was Jesus Christ on Calvary's cross. There He took our sins in His body on the tree. His crucifixion for us was a substitution so that we, in looking back to His finished work on Calvary, might confess our sins and receive repentance. Upon doing so, we then, in His forgiveness of our sin, receive Christ as our personal Savior. As the old hymn states:

> "Jesus paid it all,
> All to Him I owe.
> Sin has left its crimson stain,
> He washes white as snow."
> *Elvina Hall*

One in the Spirit

Now, as we continue our study in Romans 8:26-27, we understand the imperative of hearing from God. To do true spiritual warfare in prayer, we must agree with the will of God. It is one thing for us to see a need and pray for it, but it is something else for us to experience God's will in the matter and agree with Him. This is where all power comes from. As Jesus stood over Jerusalem, He wept. He was broken over the rejection of who He was. He cried out, "If only you would have received me." The Scriptures speak of his agony in Hebrews 5:7-8. Here Christ,

> **...while in the days of his ministry on the earth, offered up prayers and supplications with strong crying and tears unto Him that was able to save Him from death, and was heard in that He feared; Though he were a Son, yet learned he obedience by the things which he suffered.**

There are real signs that you are hearing from God in your prayers. By them you can know that God, through you, is ministering His will. First, your emotions and feelings becoming linked and coupled with the expression of God's Spirit within you. You will become broken in your praying. In fact, one sure way to know that your spirit life has become one with the Holy Spirit is that you will, in agony, grieve over the lost.

Another is that you will find yourself praying for things to which God's mind is attuned. You will know He is using you in prayer and intercession to defeat the enemy. On other occasions, you will be overwhelmed with compassion, brokenness, or joy in the matter for which you are praying. Here again is the indelible sign that you have touched the heart of God. You become one in the Spirit with Him and experience what He feels regarding what you are praying for at that time. He has consumed you and is interceding through you.

Dr. R.A. Torrey spoke of Dwight L. Moody's life this way. "I wish to testify that he was a far greater pray-er than he was a preacher. Time and time again, he was confronted by obstacles that seemed insurmountable, but he always knew the way to surmount and overcome all difficulties. He knew the way to bring to pass anything that needed to be brought to pass. He knew and believed in the deepest depths of his soul that nothing was too hard for the Lord and prayer could do anything that God could do." Few men have had the impact upon the world for the kingdom of God that Moody had. Thousands of pastors, missionaries and workers have graduated from his school in Chicago. They have taken the Gospel message around the world. This is in addition to his great impact on history as an evangelist. Hundreds of thousands found Christ as their personal savior through this man of prayer who was abandoned to God.

There is no way to express the joy that comes in the heart when you have that kind of breakthrough in prayer. You know that God has used you to bring about His will in a situation or in the life of a person. The reason such joy consumes you is that you are feeling exactly what God feels. You are *"one in the Spirit"* with Him.

"Thy kingdom come, Thy will be done, on earth as it is in heaven." This is not God just watching over His people. This is God in His people, ministering through them His will. It is already done in heaven. He performs it here through us in our obedience. Again, please remember God is not going to reward you in heaven for what you have done in Christ's name, but for what He has done through you.
This is true intercession.

—Mickey Bonner

Chapter Nine

Real Truth of Intercession

We have a spiritual infirmity which hinders our knowing the mind of God. His ways are not our ways. His language is not our language. The finite human mind does not comprehend the infinite mind and wisdom of God. So, therefore, we must seek His mind and His life with all of our heart. He must conduct His program through us. Let's return to Romans 8:26-27 in the Amplified Bible:

> **So too the [Holy] spirit comes to our aid and bears us up in our weakness; for we do not know what prayer to offer nor how to offer it worthily as we ought to, but the Spirit Himself goes to meet our supplication and pleads in our behalf with unspeakable yearnings and groanings too deep for utterance. And He who searches the hearts of men knows what is the**

mind of the [Holy] Spirit—what His intent is—because the Spirit intercedes and pleads [before God] in behalf of the saints according to and in harmony with God's will.

This passage explodes with the real truth of intercession and what it means to the believer.

In the light of this translation, join me in examining God's part in our praying. Here the Holy Spirit meets our supplication and, *"pleads in our behalf with unspeakable yearnings and groanings too deep for utterance."* This is the language of God translating His will into our heart.

For you who have wondered if you have experienced intercession, I ask you this question: Has there ever been a time when you were praying and the burden became so heavy within you that you could hardly rest until the answer came? Many times you were not even aware of what you were praying for. Because of your obedience and desire to walk with God, He found in you a vessel through whom He could minister. Therefore, He used you by bringing through you the agony of soul (groanings) necessary to bring about His will. In essence, through you, the power of the Holy Spirit defeated satan and his strongholds!

My friend, that is the epitome of all prayer. There is nothing any deeper. Oh what joy it is to be available to God, and then to be used of God as you agonize in prayer until the release comes. It is a tragedy that only a few believers ever experience this wondrous relationship with God in their lifetime.

Light

God continues then, in verse 27, *"And He Who searches the hearts of men."* Herein lies the work of the Holy Spirit. He knows what every need is. Therefore, He is constantly searching for someone who is spiritually available to show Himself strong to or through (II Chronicles 16:9). We may observe a situation in the life of an individual and by emotion pray for it. However, the root of their problem (stronghold) could be vastly different from that for which you are interceding. However, when we seek Him to find out what to pray, the Holy Spirit then intercedes and pleads through us before God on behalf of the saints. This praying is according to and in harmony with God's will. The end result is you have made yourself available to the will of God and He accomplished the intercession through His power. The truth of every matter comes to light through true intercessory praying. This is the ministry of discernment. We know not what to pray for, but the Holy Spirit does. Such is the power and glory of intercession.

The Scripture is filled with verses dealing with the issue of God performing His will through the submitted person in a powerful way. In II Kings 6:17: *"And Elijah prayed and said; Lord, open his eyes that he may see."* In verse 20: *"And Elijah said, Lord, open the eyes of these men that they may see."* God tells us in Isaiah 59:16: *"He saw that there was no man, and wondered that there was no intercessor."*

As stated earlier, the greatest intercessor in history is Jesus Christ. We find in Hebrews 7:25, *"He is able to save them to the uttermost that come unto God by Him, seeing He ever liveth to make intercession for them."* He knows totally our every need, want, and desire. He prays for us to yield to Him, knowing when we do He will be able to extend Himself through us (John 17:13). Jesus says also of our intercession, in John 16:24, 26: *"Hitherto have you asked nothing in my name: ask, and ye shall receive, that your joy may be full ...At that day, ye shall ask in my name: and I say not unto you, that I will pray the Father for you."*

Another form of intercession comes in the form of the intuitive will of God for your life. In Matthew 6, in what we call "The Lord's Prayer," He says, *"Thy kingdom come, Thy will be done, on earth as it is in heaven."* This is not God just watching over His people. This is God in His people, ministering through them His will. It is already done in heaven. He performs it here through us in our obedience. Again, please remember God is not going to reward you in heaven for what you have done in Christ's name, but for what He has done through you. This is true intercession.

God's Spirit led Paul to write the Book of Ephesians in response to his desire to serve God and to see His effective ministry through him. Never have we read anything that had a stronger appeal for and a declaration of power through the life of the believer than this epistle. Ephesians 3:16 is a statement that confirms this truth. Paul knew all true Christian ministry was Christ living through him, for he says: "I bow my knees unto the Father that He would grant thee to be strengthened by His Spirit." (You should make a study of this wonderful prayer in Ephesians 3:14-21.)

Getting Dressed for the Battle

There is another important aspect of intercession in the book of Ephesians. Here the Word teaches us that, as the Christian goes on in obedience in Christ and begins to grow in grace, the Holy Spirit covers him with armor:

> **Wherefore take unto you the whole armor of God, that ye may be able to withstand in the evil day, and having done all, to stand. Stand therefore, having your loins girt about with truth, and having on the breastplate of righteousness; and your feet shod with the preparation of the gospel of peace; above all, taking the shield of faith, wherewith ye shall be able to quench all the fiery darts of the wicked. And take the helmet of salvation, and the sword of the Spirit, which is the word of God; praying always with all prayer and supplication in the Spirit, and watching thereunto with all perseverance and supplication for all saints (Ephesians 6:13-18).**

We find every piece of armor is a derivative of the name of Jesus Christ. Contrary to most teaching of these passages, you do not personally put on the armor yourself. God places it upon the Christian in the sequence of spiritual growth and maturity. First, the belt of truth is *"gird"* or wrapped about him at salvation. Christ is our truth, as well as our way and our life.

> **Jesus said to him, I am the Way and the Truth and the Life; no one comes to the Father except by (through) Me. (John 14:6 Amplified).**

He is also our salvation.

Next, as we grow from the baby stage of hearing only voice inflection to deeper understanding and direction, we begin to realize intuitively God's daily plan for us. This comes as we begin to see the focus of our true spiritual life as we daily place ourselves in the Lord's will. He then increases us by putting the *"breastplate of righteousness"* upon us. Righteousness means "right standing with God." Stated in a different way, "standing right where God is in us." This happens in response to an act of obedience on our part.

Then, as we continue to mature, He places us into His path or will. In sequence of growth, He makes sure our feet are *"shod"* with the preparation of the *"Gospel of peace."*

The steps of a [good] man are directed and established by the Lord when He delights in his way [and He busies Himself with his every step] (Psalm 37:23 Amplified).

Just as Christ is our righteousness, so is He our peace. Peace is not an experience: it is a Person. Peace is Christ alive and living in us. As we labor to continue obeying and growing, God begins to put us in the path of His daily will so we can walk in it. All this is a process of the Savior continuing His ministry through us. As we develop spiritually, we begin to understand more deeply and fully the profound depths of Christ and His life. We are then drawn to act in believing prayer. At this point, He covers us with the *"shield of faith."*

Through the practice of prayer and hearing from God, He strengthens our faith until we *"live by the faith of the Son of God"* (Galatians 2:20). Christ becomes our faith. Better yet, Christ's faith becomes ours. At this level of growth, the shield (Christ) protects us when Satan attacks. With this protection we can now aggressively move against him. No longer will we sit passively. We refuse to let him bring us into a defensive position from which to destroy us or others for whom we are praying. No darts thrown by satan can overcome us. In fact, at this level of growth, we constantly overcome him (answered prayer). With this comprehension of Christ, we are anxious for battle. We look for a fight! As the Scriptures say, we *"watch therefore and pray."*

Also at this level of maturing, our faith becomes substance.

Now faith is the substance of things hoped for, the evidence of things not seen (Hebrews 11:1).

Having experienced this glory, we desire to put on the next piece of the Christian armor. Here He places upon us the *"helmet of salvation."* The Scripture teaches that Christ is our salvation.

For with my [own] eyes I have seen Your Salvation (Luke 2:30 Amplified).

When we have grown to this position and the helmet is placed upon us, the mind of Christ consumes and covers our minds.

Let this same attitude and purpose and [humble] mind be in you which was in Christ Jesus: [Let Him be your example in humility:]

Therefore, my dear ones, as you have always obeyed [my suggestions], so now, not only [with the enthusiasm you would show] in my presence but much more because I am absent, work out (cultivate, carry out to the goal, and fully complete) your own salvation with reverence and awe and trembling (self-distrust, with serious caution, tenderness of conscience, watchfulness against temptation, timidly shrinking from whatever might offend God and discredit the name of Christ) (Philippians 2:5; 2:12 Amplified).

As stated in Romans 12:1-2, your part is presenting your body. In this case, it is letting Christ dress you in His armor. God's part is giving you His mind when you are fully dressed (maturing). With the helmet of salvation placed over us, we are transformed by the renewing (replacing) of our minds. Now, we have the faculties to see with His eyes, and hear with His ears, and walk in His light, and stand in His faith, just as Jesus did when He walked on the earth.

I am able to do nothing from Myself [independently, of My own accord—but only as I am taught by God and as I get His orders]. Even as I hear, I judge [I decide as I am bidden to decide. As the voice comes to Me, so I give a decision], and My judgment is right (just, righteous), because I do not seek or consult My own will [I have no desire to do what is pleasing to Myself, My own aim, My own purpose] but only the will and pleasure of the Father Who sent Me (John 5:30 Amplified).

We are now a weapon in His arsenal of intercessors—"hearers." We also, at this point, see who we are in Christ and what His ministry through us is intended to be. In sequence, His personalized daily plan for us begins to manifest itself (Ephesians 2:10). We now walk in it. The process of experiencing the truth of *"work out your own salvation with fear and trembling"* (Philippians 2:12) unfolds in our lives. Salvation, in this case, is the Savior's will in the believer's life as written in heaven.

When you were a baby or adolescent you could never take responsibility. You were too young, too inexperienced. You had to be cared for rather than taking care of others. Now you are a graduate with internal knowledge in your mind. You not only understand the hard words, but now you comprehend a language. Christ has dressed Himself on you. You see His purpose and know His language. You are now ready for the final weapon of our war: the *"sword of the Spirit."* In this case, the sword is the Word of God. My beloved, Jesus Christ is the living Word.

In the beginning [before all time] was the Word (Christ), and the Word was with God, and the Word was God Himself. He was present originally with God (John 1:1-2 Amplified).

He is living His life through you (anointing). You are now all dressed up and have someplace to go.

Suddenly, the Bible is no longer mere chapter and verse, ink and page, leather cover, or translation. It now becomes the living, breathing person of Christ. His words are alive in you!

> **And having said this, He breathed on them and said to them, Receive the Holy Spirit (John 20:22 Amplified)!**

At this level of growth, we read the Word and tremble at its glory.

> **For all these things My hand has made, and so all these things have come into being [by and for Me], says the Lord. But this is the man to whom I will look and have regard: he who is humble and of a broken or wounded spirit, and who trembles at My word and reveres My commands. (Isaiah 66:2 Amplified).**

It quickens our spirit, excites our heart, and its power becomes energy in our being.

> **And what is the exceeding greatness of His power to us-ward who believe, according to the working of His mighty power (Ephesians 1:19).**

When Jesus encountered satan in the wilderness and was tempted, He destroyed his power by stating, "*It is written.*" With that admonition, the devil departed from Jesus. He was unable to overcome Christ with the sounds of the sword of the living Word piercing him. With the Word, satan was defeated then as well as he is today.

When the Word—the person of Christ—comes alive and living within you, it becomes a message and ministry of warfare. You are able to use it to destroy the kingdom of darkness. In fact, the living Word of God hidden in the heart of the Christian at this level brings the most powerful form of praying known. Intercession is God's power through man. Seek with all your heart to be covered in the armor. Make it your life's goal. It is the abundant life.

It Works

After we are dressed in Jesus, what is the next step? Here Verse 18 declares, *"...praying always with all prayer... and supplication in the Spirit and watching thereunto with all perseverance and supplication for all saints."*

Several years ago, God impressed me to write a book on the biblical teaching of the mind. The mind is the seat of all emotions and is, therefore, the battleground of life. I titled the book *God Can Heal Your Mind*. Through its content we sought to bring the reader to the place of completely forgiving all in their past. In doing so, they closed any door by which the root of bitterness had destroyed them.

> **Exercise foresight and be on the watch to look [after one another], to see that no one falls back from and fails to secure God's grace (His unmerited favor and spiritual blessing), in order that no root of resentment (rancor, bitterness, or hatred) shoots forth and causes trouble and bitter torment, and the many become contaminated and defiled by it (Hebrews 12:15 Amplified).**

Satan works in the past. God works in the present and in the future. Satan, in his effort to stop the believer's growth, will bring to a Christian constant remembrance of negative things which hinder and separate them from the will of God. The person who has bitterness and unforgiveness is spiritually crippled and defeated. He spends all his time battling emotional problems. To be dressed in righteousness, there must be the inward act of forgiving all who have trespassed against you—no matter who or what the circumstance.

> **For if you forgive people their trespasses— that is, their reckless and willful sins, leaving them, letting them go and giving up resentment—your heavenly Father will also forgive**

you. But if you do not forgive others their trespasses—their reckless and willful sins, leaving them, letting them go and giving up resentment—neither will your Father forgive you your trespasses (Matthew 6:14-15, Amplified).

Once the believer has become transparent through open confession, he will hear from God. He promises this in James 5:16.

Confess your faults one to another, and pray one for another, that ye may be healed. The effectual fervent prayer of a righteous man availeth much.

In your cleansed state, your praying becomes *"effectual"* (God praying to God). You no longer pray in generalities or recite memorized appeals such as, "Now I lay me down to sleep." You begin to pray fervently or aggressively without fear. That kind of praying "avails much" (James 5:16). Better said, that kind of praying makes all of God available through you at the level of your faith. This is why you must let Christ heal your mind. The battleground is your mind. Once Christ conquers your mind the battlefield becomes prayer. Inward first; outward second. He works through you!

(For the weapons of our warfare are not carnal, but mighty through God to the pulling down of strong holds;) Casting down imaginations, and every high thing that exalteth itself against the knowledge of God, and bringing into captivity every thought to the obedience of Christ (II Corinthians 10:4-5).

All Dressed Up and Someplace to Go

Now that we are all dressed in the armor of God, we are commanded to pray (Ephesians 6:18). As we have grown *"in grace and knowledge,"* there is now constant awareness of who we are in Christ. Warriors or intercessors are made and not born. They are the result of brokenness through many encounters and battles. They are seasoned by experience to know that "*at the name of Jesus every knee shall bow*" and they enjoy the conflict. In fact, prayer is no longer a burden, but a joy. It becomes habit-forming and wondrously addictive as they desire to see what God is up to at that moment in their personal lives.

In the process of becoming mature enough to enter into the battle, the mind of Christ covers our mind as the "helmet of salvation." We are now the front line troops. With His thoughts and ways, we know who we are by knowing who He is. We enter into the warfare "*with settled and absolute knowledge that they have granted to them as their present possessions the request made of Him*" (Romans 8:27, Amplified). What an incredible promise, and it is true! However, the believer must labor for it through the schools of hearing, of understanding, and of being dressed in the armor.

Because of submission, believers are fully armed and clothed in Christ. From this place of victory, they enter the arena of prayer. Here they strip satan of his armor and come out of the encounter with the spoils of war (armor).

But when one stronger than he attacks him and conquers him, he robs him of his whole armor on which he had relied and divides up and distributes all his goods as plunder (spoil) (Luke 11:22 Amplified).

They are becoming what God had planned for them. This results only from growth in Christ. When the *"helmet of salvation"* (the mind of Christ) is placed on the heads of Christians, they see, hear, and know His will. This is God speaking to the saints to direct their steps and extend Christ's ministry through them. In essence, all that we have said and tried to imply can be simply wrapped up in one single word—intercession.

Too Little, Too Late

This is the "why?" of no revival today. God says in

Matthew 9:37-38: *"The harvest truly is plenteous, but the laborers are few; pray ye therefore to the Lord of the harvest that He will send forth laborers into His harvest."* How does revival come? Prayer (II Chronicles 7:14). How should people be selected to minister within the church? Prayer.

So pray to the Lord of the harvest to force out and thrust laborers into His harvest (Matthew 9:38 Amplified).

Prayer is critically lacking within the local church body!

I know thy works, that thou art neither cold nor hot: I would thou wert cold or hot (Revelation 3:15).

Satan has won the battle when he keeps Christians flesh-bound in the convenience of dead religions. He has destroyed the intercession of the majority of believers. Very few are truly serious about broken praying (II Chronicles 7:14, Isaiah 57:15, Isaiah 66:2). However, as God's judgment continues upon this world's system, this is radically changing. My prayer is that it will not be, for many, too little, too late.

Seek the Lord [inquire for Him, inquire of Him, and require Him as the foremost necessity of your life], all you humble of the land who have acted in compliance with His revealed will and have kept His commandments; seek righteousness, seek humility [inquire for them, require them as vital]. It may be you will be hidden in the day of the Lord's anger (Zephaniah 2:3 Amplified).

This verse in Zephaniah was given to me as I prayed regarding my children and grandchildren. I asked God to reveal to me how to pray for their future. After I received this verse, I made a study of its content and message. God overwhelmed my heart with the revelation that I must intercede for them through a broken heart. There had to be a deepening work in my own personal life. I must abandon my entire being to Christ that He might live His will through me. His commandments were to be adhered to from the inside out, reflecting a walk with God rather than an external application of principles in the flesh. Then as I pray for them in intercession *"it may be [they] will be hidden in the day of the Lord's anger."* God's judgment is already on the land. We must yield ourselves to be conformed to His will and bring ourselves to a place where we can hear His voice. Intercession is the power of the Holy Spirit's possession of our lives. For the sake of revival, we must get to a "hearing place." We must! It is our only hope.

I am reminded of one of God's greatest prayer warriors. His name was John Hyde. He had received another name from those who knew the depth of his life of prayer. He was lovingly called "Praying" Hyde. Much has been written about his life and his ability to hear from God. Dr. J. Wilber Chapman tells a story that sheds light on the power of intercession of this praying saint. Mr. Hyde had become ill in India and was returning home to America. He stopped in England to visit fellow missionaries. Dr. Chapman was conducting revival services in Shrewsbury, England. God's Spirit was not moving in power. The numbers attending were small. While in England, John Hyde was directed by the Holy Spirit to pray for the meetings in Shrewsbury. Dr. Chapman said this regarding the results as "Praying" Hyde interceded for his ministry:

> Almost instantly the tide turned. The hall was packed, and my first invitation meant fifty men for Jesus Christ. As we were leaving I said, "Mr. Hyde, I want you to pray for me." He came to my room, turned the key in the door, dropped on his knees, waited five minutes without a single syllable coming from his lips. I could hear my own heart thumping and beating. I felt the hot tears running down my face. I knew I was with God. Then with upturned face, down which the tears were streaming, he said: "Oh, God!"
>
> Then for five minutes at least, he was still again, and then when he knew he was walking with God,

his arm went around my shoulder and there came up from the depth of his heart such petitions for men as I had never heard before. I rose from my knees to know what real prayer was. (Edman)

John Hyde moved into Gods presence, heard His will and stood in faith until it was done. This is God's power through man—true intercessory prayer.

When Jesus rose from the grave, He led
captivity captive. He destroyed completely
the power of death. He reigns now as
righteous King for all eternity. We who
have been saved are not only His subjects,
but we have living within us the majesty
of His life and being. Therefore we are
His ambassadors. We are the godly
representatives of His Kingdom
—Mickey Bonner

Chapter Ten

Hearing the Voice of God

As we continue to greater understanding of the voice of God, we find Colossians 4:2-3 tells us what to do to operate in His power. It says, *"Continue in prayer, and watch in the same with thanksgiving, praying also for us."* When you have the mind of God in a matter and you pray it, you will then experience peace within that it is done. As Jeremiah 33:3 says: *"Call unto me and I will answer thee."* With the knowledge that you are praying His will and that God is hearing and will answer, you stand in thanksgiving that it is being answered. This praise is faith affirmation.

This is, again, the message of Hebrews 11. Those living by faith received a report. Though they had not seen with their eyes, they all received and stood in faith believing. They heard "yes" in their spirit and rejoiced. Later, the report they received came to pass. This is the *"substance"* of Hebrews 11:1: *"Now faith is the substance of things hoped for, the evidence of things not seen."* Though we do not see it with our eyes, having heard from God, we know it to be so, therefore it will come to pass.

As mentioned earlier, in Psalm 37:4 God says, *"Delight thyself in the Lord, and He shall give thee the desires of thine heart."* This is also a door to intercession. We bring ourselves to Him so we can hear His *"still small voice."* This is God speaking to us His will. In the process, we agree with Him; and because we delight in Him more than anything else, the Spirit of God begins pouring His life and will through us. We are the connecting force.

We can illustrate this with the example of an electrical lamp. In order for you to bring light to your home you must have electricity to make it work. There must be a cord to extend from the unit to the power source for the light to burn. In this matter of God's life flowing, we are that cord. In fact, prayer is God's power through man. His part is the energy; our part is to "plug in." As a result God's life flows, and His light shines, through us.

In essence, all true ministry or life totally depends upon our maturity in Christ. The imperative is to hear and understand His voice within, and then to obey Him. Today's terrible tragedy is that the standard of success in Christianity has become equated to the size of the church and the amount of the offering. Many pastors today, as in the corporate world, plan their future and then work their plan. They climb the ladder of success based on the traditions of man. Churches choose pastors as builders rather than as men broken before God.

One of God's best known evangelists of the 20th century always counteracted the tribute paid to him. People would say, "When you stand before God, your reward will be great for all the souls that have found eternal presence with God because of your ministry." His reply, in essence, was, "No, the greatest reward will probably be to some individual who spent a lifetime in intercession and, through their prayers, the power of God fell."

The Mountain Top

We must be able to hear from God to fulfill His will and obey His commands. The Scripture emphasizes that the key to all prayer is hearing. In a parable in

Matthew 7:24-27, Jesus says:

> **"Everyone therefore who hears these my words and acts upon them, shall be likened to a wise man who built his house on rock. And the rain fell, and the floods came, and the winds blew and beat against that house, but it did not fall, because it was founded on rock. And everyone who hears these my words and does not act upon them, shall be likened to a foolish man who built his house on sand. And the rain fell, and the floods came, and the winds blew and beat against that house, and it fell, and was utterly ruined."**

True relationship with God is hearing in the *"hidden man of the heart"* (I Peter 3:4). Regarding this, Christ speaks about the wise man who built his house upon the rock. He begins the verse by saying that those who hear these things and do them are men with wisdom. All true ministry is predicated on hearing. This means hearing by revelation. We do not hear truth with the ear, but rather with the heart. Regardless of what comes against him, whether it be rain, or flood, or even the winds of doubt, one who hears will stand fast. When the Christian responds to the voice of God's will, *"no weapon formed against them will prosper."* The Amplified translation of Isaiah 54:17 says...

> **But no weapon that is formed against you shall prosper, and every tongue that shall rise against you in judgment you shall show to be in the wrong. This [peace, righteousness, security, triumph over opposition] is the heritage of the servants of the Lord [those in whom the ideal Servant of the Lord is reproduced]; this is the righteousness or the vindication which they obtain from Me [this is that which I impart to them as their justification], says the Lord.**

He will stand. He will not fall. Through this parable,

Christ illustrates a vital principle. We must be founded upon Him, Jesus, as the rock.

However, if we do not obey what we hear within or through the Word by inspiration, we will begin to structure our lives, or even our ministries, upon sand. Sand is the low land. It is the easy way. We do not have the strain of carrying the weighty materials up the mountain. There is no effort or struggle. There is no real need for perseverance or prayer. This is the religion of today. It is the easy way. Because men have built on satan's soil, it is easy for his flooding elements of discouragement and fear to continually wash them away.

All true foundations are laid by prayer and Bible study. Upon these we erect the structures of life and ministry after we experience brokenness before God. However, if we have built on sand, tribulation comes and begins to make the river of doubt swell, and strikes the edifice and destroys it. Then satan amplifies the falling by constant accusation. Christians become more and more discouraged, despondent, and saturated with fear. Finally, they come to the conclusion, "I must not have faith." Consequently they live in defeat. However, those who have built on the rock will get excited when troubles come and will praise in adversity.

> **Consider it wholly joyful, my brethren, whenever you are enveloped in or encounter trials of any sort or fall into various temptations. Be assured and understand that the trial and proving of your faith bring out endurance and steadfastness and patience. But let endurance and steadfastness and patience have full play and do a thorough work, so that you may be [people] perfectly and fully developed [with no defects], lacking in nothing (James 1:2-4 Amplified).**

Beloved, build your life on the rock. And as the song says:

> "This rock is Jesus, He is the one.
> This rock is Jesus, the only one.
> Be very sure, be very sure,

Your anchor holds and grips the
solid rock."

Jesus concludes this parable with the statement that
those who build on sand are foolish. They have denied the
Word from God and will perish. Such is the religious, carnal,
Laodician life of today (Revelation 3). They built their works
on sand, so their works will be burned up in the judgment.

Then, in Matthew 7:29, we find, *"For He taught them as
one having authority and not as the scribes."* These teachings startled those who were listening. They had built their
entire religious experience around the Law. They were
experts at taking the Word of God and adding to it the concepts of man. It is the same in America today. There are
thousands of religious sects and denominations, and the
number is growing. These organizations begin with a message. From there, they evolve into ministries. Then after
years of self-promulgation, they settle into being monuments, and become battlefields over the truth of their own
doctrine. Incidentally, monuments are usually testimonies
to those who were formerly alive.

In the case of those who have built on the rock, Jesus
says, *"All authority is given unto Me under heaven and
earth"* (Matthew 28:18). That authority is the person of
Christ who lives within us. As believers, the practice of
prayer and being broken before God transforms us and we
operate by the power of the Holy Spirit (Romans 12:2). He
ministers His authority through our lives by prayer. This is
the difference between being on sinking sand and the solid
rock. Besides that, the vision is always the best from the
mountain top. To be next to Christ and able to hear His
voice is to be aware spiritually that we are seated in the
heavenlies.

**And [so that you can know and understand]
what is the immeasurable and unlimited and
surpassing greatness of His power in and for
us who believe, as demonstrated in the working of His mighty strength, which He exerted
in Christ when He raised Him from the dead
and seated Him at His [own] right hand in the**

heavenly [places] (Ephesians 1:19-20 Amplified).

Born a King

A man may be born a king over a country, but at his birth he is just a baby. He must be tended to, cared for, and nurtured. In the growing days of his young life he learns obedience. Then, one day he discovers his authority as those around him continually pay homage to him. This begins the transition of his lifestyle toward his monarchy. In the meantime, his education and care include all the amenities of his throne rights. Then, as he continues to grow, he becomes more and more aware of who he is. One day, with great pomp and circumstance, the crown is placed upon his head. He has entered his sovereignty as monarch of his land.

When Jesus rose from the grave, He led captivity captive. He destroyed completely the power of death. He reigns now as righteous King for all eternity. We who have been saved are not only His subjects, but we have living within us the majesty of His life and being. Therefore, we are His ambassadors. We are the godly representatives of His kingdom. When we walk into any situation through prayer and by spiritual direction, The Lord Christ represents all that He is through us. Then, in turn, in an ambassadorial position, we represent the covenant of heaven and extend its powers. For all of this to happen through us, we must be able to hear and understand the Spirit's voice within. This comes only from the warfare of being in the school of prayer on a constant, day-by-day basis. We live in the process of learning to hear and understand His voice as we grow in grace and knowledge. As we mature mentally and spiritually, we begin to understand and exercise our throne rights. We discover daily who we are and what we are in Christ.

Over and over in the New Testament we read the statement: *"He who has an ear, let him hear."* This means he who can hear and understand the language of God. To come to this place is a battle against our own flesh. Flesh and self must be conquered and presented back to God. So few ever stay in the battle. Therefore, they live defeated, desolate, satan-dominated lives. They spend all their Christian life rebuilding their homes (lives) on the easy sand. We call this "rededication." Better said, this is the believer's "weekly New Year's resolutions."

God still speaks to His church today, but due to an infantile, immature, baby, milk-fed Christianity, much of it cannot hear and understand, much less recognize and obey Him. Only the believers who will submit to Christ and be filled with His Spirit will begin that journey. We have stated many times in this book, that as a Christian you must have a driving force within, pressing you to study and pray. You must couple this with presenting yourself daily as a living sacrifice. This will bring you into fellowship with the Holy Spirit and recognition that you belong to God. Then, as you grow, you will begin to see His majesty and might. He will begin to minister through your life as He meets your needs supernaturally. Through these experiences, your faith will increase and grow. God will continually prepare you to perform greater works of ministry!

This also is the process of His placing the armor on you and fitting it piece-by-piece (Ephesians 6:10-18). The medieval knights had to wear their armor constantly. In the process, its weight and bulk became a natural part of their body movement. You, too, become joyously accustomed to the Savior as He becomes one with your body—not only physically, but in your spirit man. You become one with the armor!

From that place, a unique experience happens to the growing believer which we find in John 16:13-14. The Amplified Bible has the best translation of these verses. It says:

"But when He, the Spirit of Truth [the truth-giving Spirit] comes, He will guide you into all the truth—the whole, full truth. For He will not speak His own message—on His own authority—but He will tell whatever He hears [from the Father, He will give the message that has been given to Him] and He will announce and declare to you the things that are to come—that will happen in the future. He will honor and glorify Me, because He will

take of [receive, draw upon] what is Mine and reveal [declare, disclose, transmit] it to you.

God will speak directly and intuitively to and through your spirit and you will begin to grow within *"in grace and knowledge."*

Here you are able to stay in prayer to the point of release, or peace, within your spirit. God says, in Luke 18:1, that you are to *"pray until the answer comes."* The Greek word used here is *"ekkakeo."* It means here not to lack courage, or lose heart or to be faint hearted. You are to stay in prayer with God until that peace, release, promise, or answer comes in your spirit as He answers speedily.

I tell you that he will avenge them speedily. Nevertheless when the Son of man cometh, shall he find faith on the earth (Luke 18:8)?

With this resolve, God will finally say to you, "It is done." To begin the ministry of warfare intercession, I urge people to pray for a single thing at a time. They are to persist until God responds in their spirit and says it is complete. When the answer comes, the Holy Spirit will have broken satan's hold in the matter for which you have prayed.

But even if our Gospel (the glad tidings) also be hidden (obscured and covered up with a veil that hinders the knowledge of God), it is hidden [only] to those who are perishing and obscured [only to those who are spiritually dying and veiled [only] to those who are lost. For the god of this world has blinded the unbelievers' minds [that they should not discern the truth], preventing them from seeing the illuminating light of the Gospel of the glory of Christ (the Messiah), Who is the Image and Likeness of God (II Corinthians 4:3-4 Amplified).

When the resistance is gone, the answer has come.

So be subject to God. Resist the devil [stand firm against him], and he will flee from you

(James 4:7 Amplified).

Peace, Be Still

When I first became a Christian, my transition to that glorious event of salvation was through the door of deep conflict. So much filth and perversion had been a part of my mental life that satan would attack my mind with thoughts and memories of past events. However, a few weeks after my conversion, God led me to a little tract I picked up somewhere while in the military. I do not remember its complete content, but there were two verses in it that I memorized. One was II Timothy 1:7, *"For God hath not given us the spirit of fear, but of power and of love and of a sound mind."* I had no idea of the depth of its meaning. However, I did know when these thoughts would come, that if I would begin to quote that Scripture over and over in my mind, I would have peace. Then I would do the same with the other verse: *"Peace I leave with thee. My peace I give unto thee, not as the world giveth unto thee. Let not your heart be troubled, neither let it be afraid"* (John 14:27). God would again cleanse my mind when I used this verse as an offensive weapon. He would always bring freedom within my spirit.

It was not long until I began to sense that, by aggressively attacking these thoughts with the Word, I was capturing and overcoming them with Scripture.

For though we walk (live) in the flesh, we are not carrying on our warfare according to the flesh and using mere human weapons. For the weapons of our warfare are not physical [weapons of flesh and blood], but they are mighty before God for the overthrow and destruction of strongholds. [Inasmuch as we] refute arguments and theories and reasonings and every proud and lofty thing that sets itself up against the [true] knowledge of God; and we lead every thought and purpose away captive into the obedience of Christ (the Messiah, the Anointed One) (II Corinthians 10:3-5 Amplified),

Not only was peace entering my mind and spirit, but something else profound was happening. Please understand that I did not use them as a defense position or simply to escape a problem. God had already shown me that the Word is a sword and a power by which we are to conquer.

For the Word that God speaks is alive and full of power [making it active, operative, energizing, and effective]; it is sharper than any two-edged sword, penetrating to the dividing line of the breath of life (soul) and [the immortal] spirit, and of joints and marrow [of the deepest parts of our nature, exposing and sifting and analyzing and judging the very thoughts and purposes of the heart (Hebrews 4:12 Amplified).

With this in mind, I would attack the evil thoughts with these truths. Then would come a peace, not only in my thoughts, but a wonderful presence of God in my life. It was as if I had been released from a bondage. Later, I discovered that I was. Oh, the joy to know that, no matter what I was facing, there was always peace to help in the midst of the storm.

He maketh the storm a calm, so that the waves thereof are stilled (Psalm 107:29).

When Jesus said, *"Peace be still,"* it was. Glory! Now, what I was doing was not meditation, though God tells us to meditate on His Word. It was focusing in faith upon the power of the Word of God. Through that process God would invoke the Holy Spirit into my life. No one had instructed me to do this to get peace within. The Holy Spirit guided me *"into all truth."* He will guide you as well. Listen to Him. If you cannot hear, force yourself to seek Him until you begin to grow in Him. As a sheep, you can and will hear His voice.

Conviction

Paul wrote the following in Romans 14:23: (quoting from the Amplified Bible)

But the man who has doubts—misgivings, an uneasy conscience—about eating, and then eats [perhaps because of you] stands condemned [before God], because he is not true to his convictions and he does not act from faith for whatever does not originate and proceed from faith is sin—that is, whatever is done without a conviction of its approval by God is sinful.

Conviction is the voice of the Holy Spirit to the heart of the believer. If you are doing things you know are wrong and there is no conviction in your spirit man, it is very likely that you have never been born again. You do them without burden. Then, if there is no move of God on your life through chastisement or corrective discipline by God, it is evident that you are lost. You must test the state of your soul. God will chasten those He loves who continue in sin. By His own Word, He states, *"If you be without chastisement, whereof all are partakers, then are you bastards and not sons."* (Hebrews 12:6-8). God's discipline is evidence of sonship.

If you are a believer and you enter into something that is not right, God will break you if you are born again. That is the result of the Father dealing with the small, immature child. He will discipline you with the many options at His disposal. Circumstances, health, depression, using the weaknesses or sins of others are all in His power to use to discipline you.

As you grow in grace and knowledge through the power of the Word, revelation then comes to your spirit by the Spirit of God. He speaks to your mind and heart and you know much more strongly within that a matter is right or wrong. The view becomes more profound as you climb (grow) the mountain (His will). It is up to you to respond accordingly. However, if you rebel while God is saying "no" to your spirit, He will then let you pass on through into darkness. In the process of spiritual failure, you will move into a tragic dimension: First, separation from the presence of God, and second, because you are out of voice range, no revelation. The Scriptures speak of this as a falling away. In the process of the climb, you slip over a cliff. Incidentally, if that has happened to you, never forget you can immediately start the climb again. God always forgives the broken, repentant heart which is ready to begin the journey upward at a moment's notice.

Sour Grapes

This reminds me of a personal incident years ago related by a great Bible teacher of my day, who has had a marked impact on my life.

A church in Florida had lost its pastor who had moved to a large church in Memphis, Tennessee. This church was formerly pastored by a great old warrior of the faith, Dr. R. G. Lee, who wrote the foreword of my first book. This great loss deeply hurt the people in Florida, however, they knew their pastor had obeyed God in the move. So, they formed a pulpit committee and soon came together praying. Seriousness prevailed as they sought God for his replacement. They were looking for a man who would be at the same spiritual walk as the godly man they lost to the Memphis church.

There was a member of that church who had been listening to tapes of a well-known evangelist. She passed them around to the pulpit committee. As they listened, they heard the depth of this man's Bible knowledge, plus the inspiration and power of God's Spirit upon him. All felt that they should at least contact him and ask if he might come to their church as a candidate. This church had achieved a name for itself through the wonderful leadership of its former pastor and the anointing was upon its people. It was well known for its ministry to the city.

So, the evangelist accepted the invitation and preached for the church. The response was overwhelming—"He's our man" was the consensus. Incidentally, the tape that opened the door for his coming to this church was titled "How to Know God's Will." With this wonderful inspired sermon and his visit still fresh in the minds of the committee, they extended a unanimous call to this man to be their pastor. After long deliberation, he said yes. He felt this was the place that God would have him continue his ministry.

Then something happened. After several weeks, the church received word from the evangelist that he had made a mistake and did not feel led of God to come. Predictably, the response of the church was great disappointment.

Later, after a period of time, one individual in that church decided to respond to this evangelist who had said, "Yes, I will come; God is leading me there," and then later rescinded that position. They sent to him a copy of his own tape on "How to Know God's Will." Now, I do not believe there were "sour grapes" involved in the sending of the message, but I have often laughed at that story, knowing this Bible teacher and his incredible walk with God. Somehow, the voice he heard to begin with was not the voice he heard later as he deliberated. It all boiled down to the fact that, in his heart, he wanted to leave the constant traveling of itinerant evangelism and pastor the church. But, in his spirit, God was saying, "Your call is evangelism."

How many times do we operate on emotion? That church was a great opportunity. It had a potential for growth, good buildings, and incredible possibilities. So, he said, based on what he felt, "This must be the will of God." However, in this case, it was not. I know this godly brother, and I know ultimately he heard and obeyed God, having seen the results of his continued ministry over the years.

God will speak to you. He will direct you. He will do it in such a way that you will know it is Christ who is working. When in that place, you are, in God's timing, to operate boldly. God will set a direction for you in His will. However, you must not try to engineer it. You must wait for God's timing and for Him to open the doors.

Many times in my ministry I have started down a road that I felt would bring great glory to the name of God. Also, if it succeeded, it would also give fame to my own name. (I suspect this was my strongest motivation at the time.) The processes would open even greater doors for me in my own personal ministry. God knew pride was welling up within me. Had He done what I desired for Him to do, I would have been another casualty on the side of the road stating, "If it were not for me, God could not have done ..." (Job 29). Again, I would say *Oh, wretched man that I am* (Romans 7:24). But I learned in the process what a wonderful Lord we serve. We can trust and wait on Him in any circumstance. He is able!!

The Spirit and the Word must be combined. If I look to the Spirit alone without the Word, I lay myself open to great delusions, also. If the Holy Spirit guides us, He will do it according to the Scriptures, never contrary to them... I take into account providential circumstances. These often plainly indicate God's will in connection with His Word and Spirit... I then ask God in prayer to reveal His will to me... Thus through prayer, the study of the Word and reflection, I come to a deliberate judgment according to the best of my ability and knowledge. If my mind is thus at peace and continues so after two or three more petitions, I proceed accordingly. I have found this method always effective in trivial or important issues.

— George Mueller

Chapter Eleven

The Will of God in Prayer

Probably the questions most asked regarding the will of God are: "How do you know what to pray for?" and, "How do you know when you have heard from God?" You must understand that God answers no prayers but His own. In Matthew 6, in what we call "The Lord's Prayer," we find the Scripture teaches *Thy kingdom come, Thy will be done on earth as it is in Heaven.*" We can best describe the kingdom of God that we are to "seek first" as God's will for our life as He has written it in heaven. This becomes personal as we understand God has a plan and a purpose for our life on a daily basis.

We have already dealt with this truth from Ephesians 2:10 in other places in this writing. This verse shows that every day of the Christian's life has already been written out. We join ourselves to this will of God by prayer if it is to become reality in our lives.

Our submission to Him through prayer and Bible study follows our analogy of a child's stages of growth on into

189

school. While a child is at home, he learns from his parents' daily instruction. This includes such facts as colors, numbers, and letters. They begin to understand simple sentence structure from the limited vocabulary they have developed to this point of life. Also by this time, a pattern of "dos and don'ts," or what is right and what is wrong, has begun to evolve from his parental environment. While the child is in his family relationship, deeper elements of character begin to formulate in his mind based upon the instruction received. This is the process of growing up.

As you study the Bible, you will discover that God, through His Spirit, always speaks to us at the level of our spiritual growth. If we are babies, we understand only the milk message. However, if we press our desire to go on with the Lord by forcing ourselves to study, pray, and fast, we soon find ourselves advancing to higher grade levels. From the first grade with its ABCs and its two–plus–twos, the teaching moves us on into higher areas of learning. This produces the greater mental growth that makes us able to grasp the more profound concepts of math and science.

In our growing education as believers, we constantly receive information. However, there is no basis for growth unless we apply the information through daily practice. I may read a book about flying a plane. I may even receive instructions about flying; but until I get into the aircraft and begin a "hands-on" experience, my information has little practical effect.

This same principle applies to personal prayer. We assimilate what we learn at the level of our spiritual maturity through discernment. From this position, we move into active and productive prayer and power. This, is all based on the level of our Christian walk (maturity) at the time we receive His revelation (teaching).

To continue with our analogy of scholastic growth, we receive teaching based on our current grade level. If we have a hunger to learn and have a real desire for education, our grades are always much better. However, if we have only a passive desire to grow, then we learn little or nothing. Our report card reads "F" or "incomplete." In this case, the "F" stands for "flesh."

But if you are guided (led) by the [Holy] Spirit, you are not subject to the law. Now the doings (practices) of the flesh are clear (obvious): they are immorality, impurity, indecency, idolatry, sorcery, enmity, strife, jealousy, anger (ill temper), selfishness, divisions (dissensions), party spirit (factions, sects with peculiar opinions, heresies) (Galatians 5:18-21 Amplified).

It is through our desire to walk with God that we continue to "grow in grace and knowledge." From there, we move from second grade, to third grade, to fourth grade, to fifth grade, and so on. Incidentally, we never graduate; we just continue to grow. A saint of the last century stated, "The world has yet to see what could happen through one person totally and completely committed to Christ." No one ever really graduates.

When an individual yields his seeking heart to the Lord Jesus, then the Holy Spirit, begins to minister the will of God through him. This is the essence of true prayer. For this to happen, the believer must mature into hearing and understanding the voice of God, either through the Word of God, or intuitively in the spirit. The prayerful ingestion of the Bible through continual study brings the voice of God within. *"Thy word have I hid in my heart that I may not sin against thee"* (Psalm 119:11).This is ingesting the Word, taking it within, like a child growing up and coming to the knowledge of right and wrong.

Nine-Tenths

There are several distinct ways to bring yourself into a hearing relationship with God, thereby being able to hear and know what to pray. Remember, prayer is not the position of the body, but the condition of the heart in responding to the Holy Spirit's directing from the inside out. I cannot say often enough: Christ's continuing ministry is prayer through the Christian. That is why God is looking for those who will listen rather than speak.

George Mueller, whom we mentioned earlier, was perhaps one of the greatest men of prayer in the last two centuries.

He had a distinct way by which he brought himself into hearing distance of the voice of God. He stated:

> Number one, I seek to get my heart into such a state that it has no will of its own in a given matter. When we are ready to do the Lord's will, whatever it may be, nine–tenths of the difficulties are overcome. Number two, having done this, I do not leave the result to feeling or simple impression. If I do so, I make myself liable to great delusions. Number three, I seek the will of the Spirit of God through, or in connection with, God's Word.
>
> THE SPIRIT AND THE WORD MUST BE COMBINED, [Mueller's emphasis.] If I look to the Spirit alone without the Word, I lay myself open to great delusions. If the Holy Spirit guides us, He will do it according to the Scriptures, never contrary to them. Number four, I take into account providential circumstances. These often plainly indicate God's will in connection with His Word and Spirit. Number five, I ask God in prayer to reveal His will to me. Number six, thus through prayer, the study of the Word and reflection, I come to a deliberate judgment according to the best of my ability and knowledge. If my mind is thus at peace and continues so after two or three more petitions, I proceed accordingly. I have found this method always effective in trivial or important issues.

This is a classic example of presentation over transformation equals God's will (P/T=GW).

When in Doubt—Don't

The thrilling light of these statements reminds me of the greatest man of faith I have ever known. His name was Manley Beasley. Manley had a saying that captured my heart years ago and I have tried to obey it: "When in doubt, don't!" If I move toward a thing and there is doubt within—and something is saying no—I back away. God will speak to you intuitively, and, beloved, He will direct your steps. The Bible says, in Proverbs 3:5-6, *"Trust in the Lord with all thine heart; and lean not unto thine own understanding. In all thy ways acknowledge Him, and He shall direct thy paths."* What an incredible promise from God!

There are three interesting Hebrew words involved in these two verses. Number one, in verse 5, the word *"understanding"* is from the word *"binā."* It is actually from the root, in the Hebrew, meaning "prudence, insight, wisdom." In essence, God is saying we are not to actively pursue life on our own mentality. He declares we must place ourselves in the wisdom of His purpose and will. We achieve this through prayer and Bible study that bring us revelation within our understanding. As we have seen so often in this book, every day of your life is already written out and you are to join God in His plan (Ephesians 2:10). Beloved, that is wisdom and insight into God's kind of life.

Then Verse 6 of Proverbs 3 begins: *"... in all thy ways acknowledge Him."* The second word that I want you to see is "in." The meaning here is to be "in God." That means a daily filling of the Spirit as you involve God in everything you are doing. When you become self-confident or self-sufficient, you deny the presence of Christ's authority in your life. This is rebellion and you have turned away from the light. You have chosen to leave the God-ordained path of righteousness He has laid out for *"His name's sake."*

Remember, religion is the activity of Christians doing Christian activity based on the concepts of man. Christianity is the activity of Christ, through man, as the Holy Spirit develops within that individual the glorious presence of Jesus Christ. True Christianity is inside out. All religion is outside in. Within its confines, you must conform yourself to a dogma, ritual, and/or tradition. Then you must work within those denominational, structured parameters by the efforts of the flesh. That makes you, in the sight of those living within that false mold, a "true Christian."

Finally, if we will do these things listed in Proverbs 3:5-6, the promise comes, *"and He shall direct thy paths."* The third Hebrew word I want to point out is *"yāsar,"* which means "to direct or to be straight, level, right, go straight." The ultimate truth of this is, as you yield to God the first place in your life, He gives to you His will. In fact, from this position in sentence structure, the word *"yāsar"* can mean "to rightly divide, to approve, make pleasing."

The whole concept here comes from *"rightly dividing the word of truth"* as we find it in II Timothy 2:15.

> **Study and be eager and do your utmost to present yourself to God approved (tested by trial), a workman who has no cause to be ashamed, correctly analyzing and accurately dividing—rightly handling and skillfully teaching —the Word of Truth (Amplified).**

To "divide" (revelation) means the Holy Spirit will direct you and *"guide you into all truth"* as you study His Word with prayer. The Greek word in this case is *"ortho-tomeo"* or to cut straight or to handle right. Biblical truth must be correctly divided–prophetically and historically–and with constant awareness of the subjects with which a passage is actually dealing. You must study the Word not only academically, but with great prayer so God can reveal His meaning for application in your life. Someone has quipped, "If you get three theologians together, you're going to have four opinions." That is true <u>except</u> where the Holy Spirit has broken into the lives of the believers and has directed them to the truth of what God has written in His Word.

Proverbs 3:5-6 from the Amplified Bible is well thought through theologically. I believe it was given with inspiration to the translator. It states:

> **Lean on, trust and be confident in the Lord with all your heart and mind, and do not rely on your own insight or understanding. In all your ways know, recognize and acknowledge Him, and He will direct and make straight and plain your paths.**

New City

The *Back to the Bible* radio broadcast brought out a little booklet titled *Guidance* by James H. McConkey. It speaks about a verse we have covered in detail throughout this book, but what it says is appropriate here. He writes of Romans 12:1 that we must be completely involved in God's will and purpose, for when we do, we operate from a promise. We find this truth also in Psalms 32:8, *"I, the Lord, will instruct you and teach you in the way you should go; I will counsel you with My eye upon you."* When we present our bodies as a living sacrifice back to God, Romans 12:2 distinctly tells us that He will transform us by the renewing of our minds. That renewal, again, is His mind over ours. From that position comes the reality of I Thessalonians 4:3 which says, *"This is the will of God, even your sanctification."*

McConkey brings something out in this little book that I totally agree with concerning praying for people. He tells about a European pastor named Blumhardt and how God greatly used him in prayer for the healing of the sick. When he first was introduced to this ministry by the Holy Spirit, he would spend a great deal of time waiting on God for a word for that individual before he would pray with anyone. Finally, when God gave him His mind in the matter, then he would pray for that person and the Lord would bring healing. Later, as he continued to do this, he discovered that the length of time between the seeking of God and the praying was shortened. This responsiveness grew until finally he could pray for an individual and, in the process of that prayer, God would immediately reveal to him the need. This is true discernment.

Some years ago, we hired a very fine man to run our ministry. His name is Don Smith. I had known Don for years and felt strongly impressed that he was to be a part of what we were doing. When he arrived to begin his work in our office, he brought with him a local map. For the next several days, everywhere we went, Don had that map out tracing where he was and where he was going. Before several weeks were over, he was as familiar with our neighborhood as I was after having lived there for twenty years. He began by asking and seeking directions, and then looked for it on that piece of paper. Later on, he knew our area intuitively and when someone would ask him about a location, he would instantly know where it was. Why? He had consulted the map. What is our map? The Word of God. What is our voice? The response to prayer from the Holy Spirit. *"Ask and ye shall receive."*

Prayer is the essential element of hearing from God. J. Wilber Chapman tells the story of Jonathan Edwards of New England as he prepared his message "Sinners in the Hands of an Angry God." Edwards was devoted to Christ from childhood. When they could not find him they knew he was in the field walking and talking with God. He was in a hearing place with God. The Holy Spirit brought a great burden to this young preacher for revival. Chapman stated that as he delivered his famous sermon, "he had a little manuscript which he held up so close to his face that the congregation could not see his countenance. But as he went on, the people in the crowded church were tremendously moved. One man sprang to his feet, rushed down the aisles, and cried, 'Mr. Edwards, have mercy!'"

Other men caught hold of the backs of the pews lest they should slip into perdition. I have seen the old pillars around which they threw their arms, when they thought the day of judgment had dawned upon them. The power of that sermon is still felt in the United States today. But there is a history behind it. For three days, Edwards had not eaten a mouthful of food, for three nights he had not closed his eyes in sleep.

Over and over again, he had been saying to God; "Give me New England! Give me New England!" and when he rose from his knees, and made his way into the pulpit they say that he looked as if he had been gazing straight into the face of God. They say that before he opened his lips to speak, conviction fell upon his audience. It is evident that Jonathan Edwards truly had God's will in his life through prayer.

Another Spirit

It is imperative for you to discern the difference between the Holy Spirit and the unholy spirit. There are spirits in the world today that are not only religious, but even take the name of Jesus. You will find this revealed in II Corinthians 11:3-4, as well as verses 12-15.

But I fear, lest by any means, as the serpent beguiled Eve through his subtlety, so your minds should be corrupted from the simplicity that is in Christ. For if he that cometh preacheth another Jesus, whom we have not preached, or if ye receive another spirit, which ye have not received, or another gospel, which ye have not accepted, ye might well bear with him (II Corinthians 11:3-4).

But what I do, that I will do, that I may cut off occasion from them which desire occasion; that wherein they glory, they may be found even as we. For such are false apostles, deceitful workers, transforming themselves into the apostles of Christ. And no marvel; for satan himself is transformed into an angel of light. Therefore it is no great thing if his ministers also be transformed as the ministers of righteousness; whose end shall be according to their works (II Corinthians 11:12-15).

God also says to try the spirits whether they are of God:

Beloved, do not trust every spirit but test the spirits to see whether they belong to God, because many false prophets have gone out into the world (I John 4:1).

Satan's ministry is to separate, deceive, and lead astray. Therefore, we must be able to recognize the true voice of God. Again, it all comes back to hearing and understanding. The Word states, *"My sheep, hear My voice."* I know instantly when my wife, son, daughter, daughter-in-law, or close friends call me on the telephone—I recognize their voice. By the same token, as you have more association with God in prayer and study, you will know when the Holy Spirit speaks to you. You must also be careful that you do not follow the wrong voice. It is just like training a child not to speak to strangers. You will hear God's voice within. You will know when a thing is wrong. I would recommend very strongly for those who are serious and want to go on with God, that you get a book entitled *The Latent Power Of The Soul*, by Watchman Nee. This will help you to understand the necessity of trying the spirits. Satan can counterfeit feelings. You must be careful, especially today.

The Holy Spirit will be your guide. If you begin a direction that you are uneasy and in doubt about, always go back to the source. Go back to the map. Go back to the Word of God and back to prayer. Listen to the voice of God that is within you. Always remember: Never "kick against the goads" and resist as the Holy Spirit leads you. Listen to your inner man, and when in doubt—don't.

Something else you must understand here is best wrapped up in an old adage: "Haste makes waste." God never hurries, but He is never late. In fact, He says in Isaiah 28:16: *"He that believeth shall not make haste."* Learn to wait upon the Lord. Then, if you find yourself going in a direction and you are uneasy about it, STOP! Wait for God. Remember always that prayer is not the position of the body, but the condition of the heart to be able to hear, to receive instruction, and to obey. The Word of God and prayer will give you the direction you must have.

The Holy Spirit spoke intuitively all through the Old Testament as God brought people to the place of ministry and service by His will. The New Testament also gives us many illustrations of God's working His will through His servants. How many times did Paul, under the leadership of the Holy Spirit, do the will of God? When he opened his mouth, he was "spoken through" with such power and glory that those around him shook in the presence of the anointing.

Then, the Spirit of God was so on Peter that even his shadow passing over the sick brought healing as his steps were ordered by the will of God. Also, Peter, at the house of Cornelius after explaining the Holy Spirit's direction in Acts 11 says, in Verse 12: *". . . and the Spirit made me go with them, nothing doubting."*

In Acts 8:26, the angel spoke to Philip's heart and brought him face to face with the Ethiopian eunuch. Verse 29 says: *"Then the Spirit said unto Philip, go near and join thyself to this chariot,"* and he did. Then, by the power of the Holy Spirit, he ministered the Word of God in glory. The man the Lord sent Philip to was born again and began his own missionary journey in Ethiopia.

One of the greatest examples of hearing from God is in the book of Revelation. The Holy Spirit anointed and gave that holy text to the mind of John for the end-times in which we live today. Another example is in Hebrew 11:8, for it speaks of Abraham and his walk with God: *"He went out, not knowing whither he went."*

The entire ministry of Jesus Christ was directed by the Father, for Jesus constantly went apart to pray to seek His will. God spoke His mind to His Son. He heard and obeyed (John 5:30). He tells us in John 20:21: *"As my father has sent me, even so I send you."*

Beloved, you can and will hear from God if you walk with Him. To have any ministry at all, we must be able to hear His voice. A statement I read several years ago has stayed with me and will not let me go. It was from the pen of Jamie Buckingham, who is now with the Lord. He said, "It's not death I fear ... Death is nothing. But to live without creating, without contributing, is to die daily." Beloved, we cannot fruitfully contribute to or continue God's ministry through us unless we can hear His voice.

Nuff Said

How often am I asked for counsel and guidance for another person's decision or direction with God. I always approach that situation with fear and trembling. My reason is that in my carnal flesh (the side of me that wants to be wise and take authority and give direction), I have a tendency to tell the individual what I would do in their case. How many times have I hurt people with this kind of counsel and guidance?

I know the Bible says that there is *"wisdom in counselors,"* and I have those whom I pray with in matters. However, it is very dangerous to place your direction in the hands of another person based on how they feel or what they think. I am more and more led to tell people that when they have a decision to make to go to the Word and then pray, asking God for direction from His inspired Scripture

in the light of their need. As they do this prayerfully, they
will encounter a Scripture passage through which God will
speak to them and quicken their heart. Their answer is
always there.

Also, they have gained two advantages from this. One,
they have gotten God's answer. Two, they have discovered
they are capable of hearing from God as He speaks to them
through the Word. It is a growing experience.

In fact, Christ emphasizes this in John 21:21 when
Peter asked Him a question, about John *"Peter seeing Him
sayeth to Jesus, Lord, and what shall this man do?"*
Christ's answer, in Verse 22, was: *"Jesus sayeth unto him,
if I will that he tarry till I come, what is that to thee? Follow
thou me."* In other words, "Mind your own business" and
wait upon the Lord and follow Him. To quote an old adage,
"nuff said."

Light a Candle

Another wonderful statement from the Word on this
truth is *"they that wait upon the Lord . . ."* We learn our
lessons by attending the class, not from hearsay. When we
present ourselves to God for an answer, He will not give us
"stone for bread." Also, while you are seeking Him, you will
learn patience waiting for the answer to come in God's timing. The Bible says, in Psalm 130:6, *"My soul waiteth for
the Lord more than they that watch for the morning; I say,
more than they that watch for the morning."* It is interesting that this verse repeats the words, *"they that watch for
the morning."* Night held only terror for those who were
unprotected and unguarded. In that desert region, it is
extremely cold after dark. As the old saying declares, "It is
better to light a candle than to curse the dark." In this case,
it is better to pray and seek God's will and wait for Hislight
to come to direct your path. He will be the lamp that will
guide your steps.

Picture in your mind the desperation of the Psalmist in
this matter. He speaks for those who desire the morning to
come so they may be able to see what is about them. Even
more so should there be desperation within our heart and
soul for the Lord. This should go beyond that of those who

tremble at every sound in the night. Oh, the joy that comes with the morning sun!—or better said, Son! Like the old hymn rejoices, "Some golden daybreak, Jesus will come."

We should desire more than anything else in this world to be able to hear from God in our spirit. For just as a watchman guards the fields, we must be willing to bring ourselves to the place of vigilance in study and prayer. We must present ourselves until we become internally sensitive to God speaking to us.

The next step is a maturing act: faithful obedience to His will. That is the process of starting to do what He designs for us to do. The imperative of the true Christian walk is His being able to continue His ministry through us according to His will. As we have said time and again in this teaching, God operates internally and intuitively and directs us in our spirit. Ask yourself these questions. Number one, "Do you hear His voice?" Number two, "If so, do you understand the language?" Read God's Word and see if He quickens you with His Spirit. Then, ask a third question, "Will you obey His voice?"

You will know when you have become a living sacrifice when He begins to tell you what to pray. The result will be the building of your faith through answered prayers. Herein is God's kingdom coming alive in you. Seek it with all of your heart.

"My sheep hear My voice ..."

Learn of Me

In the book *Brokenness: The Forgotten Factor of Prayer*, I have explained my transition to brokenness and the missed opportunities to be used of God because of my pride and the wretchedness of my life. I would pray to be used, and God would direct me to great results. Then I would stand in the midst of it and say, "Look what I've done." Nothing blocks the channel of hearing the voice of God quicker than self–glorification. Don't let this happen to you.

Learn to hear from God. Learn to discern His voice. Learn to discern His language. Learn to experience His feelings. For He says, *"Learn of me."* When this begins to happen, you will live *"thy kingdom come, thy will be done."* Then you will walk in a supernatural realm. Let Christ Jesus have your life. Abandon yourself to Him. From the depth of your soul, cry out to Him, "Oh, Lord, I want to do Your will more than anything else in my life." Then you will begin to walk in the Spirit. You will hear His voice. The result will come when you someday stand before Him in judgment. II Corinthians 5:10 states:

For we must all appear and be revealed as we are before the judgment seat of Christ, so that each one may receive [his pay] according to what he has done in the body, whether good or evil, [considering what his purpose and motive have been, and what he has achieved, been busy with, and given himself and his attention to accomplishing] (Amplified).

You will hear Him say, *"Well done, thou good and faithful servant".* This is the result of your submission to His voice. Jude, Verse 20, says:

But you, beloved, build yourselves up [founded] on your most holy faith—make progress, rise like an edifice higher and higher—praying in the Holy Spirit (Amplified).

As you pursue Christ and present yourself daily in submission to the living God, you will find yourself going higher and higher up the mountain of His will. What a breathtaking view of God's Glory! You will grow as you pray the mind of Christ. Seek Him. Allow Him to break you. Go after Him with all your heart as you declare from your heart, *"Thy will be done."*

Appendix

Charles Finney was a man totally tuned into Christ. The story of his life and ministry have impacted my own life as I have desired to walk with God. As a lawyer in the early 1800s, he surrendered his life to Christ. From then on, God ministered His life through him. Here is the profound story of his conversion and filling in his own words. This excerpt taken from *They Found The Secret* by Raymond V. Edman.

On a Sabbath evening in the autumn of 1821, I made up my mind that I would settle the question of my soul's salvation at once, that if it were possible I would make my peace with God. But as I was very busy in the affairs of the office, I knew that without great firmness of purpose, I should never effectually attend to the subject. I therefore then and there resolved, as far as possible, to avoid all business, and everything that would divert my attention, and to give myself wholly to the work of securing the salvation of my soul. I carried this resolution into execution as sternly and thoroughly as I could. I was, however, obliged to be a good deal in the office. But as the providence of God would have it, I was not much occupied either on Monday or Tuesday, and had opportunity to read my Bible and engage in prayer most of the time. . . .

During Monday and Tuesday my convictions increased; but still it seemed as if my heart grew harder. I could not shed a tear; I could not pray. I had not opportunity to pray above my breath; and frequently I felt that if I could be alone where I could use my voice and let myself out, I should find relief in prayer. I was shy, and avoided, as much as I could, speaking to anybody on any subject. I endeavored, however, to do this in a way that would excite no suspicion, in any mind, that I was seeking the salvation of my soul.

During Monday and Tuesday my convictions increased; but still it seemed as if my heart grew harder. I could not shed a tear; I could not pray. . . .

Tuesday night I had become very nervous; and in the night a strange feeling came over me as if I was about to die. I knew that if I did I should sink down to hell; but I quieted myself as best I could until morning.

At an early hour I started for the office. But just before I arrived at the office, something seemed to confront me with questions like these: indeed, it seemed as if the inquiry was within myself, as if an inward voice said to me, "What are you waiting for? Did you not promise to give your heart to God" And what are you trying to do? Are you endeavoring to work out a righteousness of your own?"

Just at this point the whole question of gospel salvation opened to my mind in a manner most marvelous to me at the time. I think I then saw, as clearly as I ever have in my life, the reality fullness of the atonement of Christ. I saw that His work was a finished work; and then instead of having, or needing, any righteousness of my own to recommend me to God, I had to submit myself to the righteousness of God through Christ. Gospel salvation seemed to me to be an offer of something to be accepted; and that it was full and complete; and that all that was necessary on my part, was to get my own consent to give up my sins, and accept Christ. Salvation, it seemed to me, instead of being a thing to be wrought out, by my own works, was a thing to be found entirely in the Lord Jesus Christ, who presented Himself before me as my God and my Saviour.

Without being distinctly aware of it, I had stopped in the street right where the inward voice seemed to arrest me. . . . [A]fter this. . . revelation had stood for some. . . time before my mind, the question seemed to be put, 'Will you accept it now, today?' I replied, 'Yes; I will accept it today, or I will die in the attempt. . . . [I]nstead of going to the office, I turned and bent my course towards the woods, feeling that I must be alone, and away from all human eyes and ears, so that I could pour out my prayer to God.

But when I attempted to pray I found that my heart would not pray. . . . When I [tried to pray], I was dumb, that is, I had nothing to say to God; or at least I could say but a few words, and those without heart. In attempting to pray I would hear a rustling in the leaves, as I thought, and would stop and look up to see if somebody were not coming. This I did several times.

At this point Finney almost fell into despair. He believed that he could not pray; that his heart was "dead to God." He began to deeply regret his promise to give himself to God before he left the woods. In prayer, he found that his "inward soul hung back," and he could not give his heart to God. He feared that it was too late for him. For some reason, God had given him up. He sensed in the depth of his being that he "was past hope" and would spend an eternity in hell. He continues the story.

The thought was pressing me of the rashness of my promise, that I would give my heart to God that day or die in the attempt. It seemed to me as if that was binding upon my soul; and yet I was going to break my vow. A great sinking and discouragement came over me, and I felt almost too weak to stand upon my knees.

Just at this moment I again thought I heard some one approach me, and I opened my eyes to see whether it were so. But right there the revelation of my pride of heart, as the great difficulty that stood in the way, was distinctly shown to me. An overwhelming sense of my wickedness in being ashamed to have a human being see me on my knees before God, took such powerful possession of me, that I cried at the top of my voice, and exclaimed that I would not leave that place if all the men on earth and all the devils in hell surrounded me. What! I said, such a degraded sinner as I am, on my knees confessing my sins to the great and holy God, and ashamed to have any human being, and a sinner like myself, find me on my knees endeavoring to make my peace with my offended God! The sin appeared awful, infinite. It broke me down before the Lord.

Just at that point this passage of Scripture seemed to drop into my mind with a flood of light: "Then shall ye go and pray unto me, and I will hearken unto you. Then shall ye seek me and find me, when ye shall search for me with all you heart" [Jeremiah 29:12-13]. I instantly seized hold of this with my heart. I had intellectually believed the Bible before; but never had the truth been in my mind that faith was a voluntary trust instead of an intellectual state. I was as conscious as I was of my existence, of trusting at that moment in God's veracity. Somehow, I knew that was a passage of Scripture, though I do not think I had ever read it. I knew that it was God's word, and God's voice, as it were, that spoke to me. I cried to Him, "Lord, I take Thee at Thy word. Now Thou knowest that I do search for Thee with all my heart, and that I have come here to pray to Thee; and Thou hast promised to hear me."

That seemed to settle the question that I could then, that day, perform my vow. The Spirit seemed to lay stress upon that idea in the text, "When you search for me with all your heart." .... I told the Lord that I should take Him at His word that He could not lie; and that therefore I was sure that He heard my prayer, and that He would be found of me....

I walked quietly toward the village; and so perfectly quiet was my mind that it seemed as if all nature listened. It was... a very pleasant day. I had gone into the woods immediately after an early breakfast; and when I returned to the village I found it was dinner time. Yet I had been wholly unconscious of the time that had passed; it appeared to me that I had been gone from the village but a short time....

I went to my dinner, and found I had no appetite to eat. I then went to the office, and found that Squire W. had gone to dinner. I took down my bass viol, and, as I was accustomed to do, began to play

and sing some pieces of sacred music. But as soon as
I began to sing those sacred words, I began to weep.
It seemed as if my heart was all liquid; and my feelings were in such a state that I could not hear my
own voice in singing without causing my sensibility
to overflow. I wondered at this, and tried to suppress
my tears, but could not. I put up my instrument and
stopped singing.

After dinner we were engaged in removing our
books and furniture to another office. We were busy
in this, and had but little conversation all the afternoon. My mind, however, remained in that profoundly tranquil state. There was a great sweetness
and tenderness in my thoughts and feelings.
Everything appeared to be going right, and nothing
seemed to ruffle or disturb me in the least.

Just before evening the thought took possession
of my mind, that as soon as I was left alone in the
new office, I would try to pray again—that . . .
although I no longer had any concern about my soul,
still I would continue to pray.

By evening, we got the books and furniture
adjusted; and I made up, in an open fireplace, a good
fire, hoping to spend the evening alone. Just at dark,
Squire W., seeing that everything was adjusted, bade
me good-night and went to his home. I had accompanied him to the door; and as I closed the door and
turned around, my heart seemed to be liquid within
me. All my feelings seemed to rise and flow out; and
the utterance of my heart was, "I want to pour my
whole soul out to God." The rising of my soul was so
great that I rushed into the room back of the front
office, to pray.

There was no fire, and no light, in the room; nevertheless it appeared to me as if it were perfectly
light. As I went in and shut the door after me, it
seemed as if I met the Lord Jesus Christ face to face.
It did not occur to me then, nor did it for some time
afterward, that it was wholly a mental state. On the
contrary, it seemed to me that I saw Him as I would
see any other man. He said nothing, but looked at

me in such a manner as to break me right down at his feet. I have always since regarded this as a most remarkable state of mind; for it seemed to me a reality, that He stood before me, and I fell down at His feet and poured out my soul to Him. I wept aloud like a child, and made such confessions as I could with a choked utterance. It seemed to me that I bathed His feet with my tears; and yet I had no distinct impression that I touched Him, that I recollect.

I must have continued in this state for a good while; but my mind was too much absorbed with the interview to recollect anything that I said. But I know, as soon as my mind became calm enough to break off from the interview, I returned to the front office, and found that the fire that I had made of large wood was nearly burned out. But as I turned and was about to take a seat by the fire, I received a mighty baptism of the Holy Ghost. Without any expectation of it, without ever having the thought in my mind that there was any such thing for me, without any recollection that I had ever heard the thing mentioned by any person in the world, the Holy Spirit descended upon me in a manner that seemed to go through me, body and soul. I could feel the impression, like a wave of electricity, going through and through me. Indeed, it seemed to come in waves and waves of liquid love; for I could not express it in any other way. It seemed like the very breath of God. I can recollect distinctly that it seemed to fan me, like immense wings.

No words can express the wonderful love that was shed abroad in my heart. I wept aloud with joy and love; and I do not know but I should say, I literally bellowed out the unutterable gushings of my heart. These waves came over me, and over me, and over me, one after the other, until I recollect I cried out, I shall die if these waves continue to pass over me. I said, "Lord, I cannot bear any more;" yet I had no fear of death.

How long I continued in this state, with this baptism continuing to roll over me and go through me, I do not know. But I know it was late in the evening when a member of my choir — for I was the leader of the choir — came into the office to see me. He was a member of the church. He found me in this state of loud weeping, and said to me, "Mr Finney, what ails you?" I could make him no answer for some time. He then said, "Are you in pain" I gathered myself up as best I could, and replied, "No, but so happy that I cannot live. . . ."

I soon fell asleep, but almost as soon awoke again on account of the great flow of the love of God that was in my heart. I was so filled with love that I could not sleep. Soon I fell asleep again and awoke in the same manner. When I awoke, this temptation would return upon me, and the love that seemed to be in my heart would abate; but as soon as I was asleep, it was so warm within me that I would immediately awake. Thus I continued till. Late at night, I obtained some sound repose.

When I awoke in the morning the sun had risen, and was pouring a clear light into my room. Words cannot express the impression that this sunlight made upon me. Instantly the baptism that I had received the night before returned upon me in the same manner. I arose upon my knees in the bed and wept aloud with joy, and remained for some time too much overwhelmed with the baptism of the Spirit to do anything but pour out my soul to God.

It seemed as if this morning's baptism was accompanied with a gentle reproof, and the Spirit seemed to say to me, "Will you doubt? Will you doubt?" I cried, "No! I will not doubt; I cannot doubt." He then cleared the subject up so much to my mind that it was in fact impossible for me to doubt that the Spirit of God had taken possession of my soul.

In this state I was taught the doctrine of justification by faith, as a present experience. That doctrine had never taken any such possession of my mind that I had ever viewed it distinctly as a fundamental doctrine of the gospel. Indeed, I did not know at all what it meant in the proper sense. But I could now see and understand what was meant by the passage, "Being justified by faith, we have peace with God through our Lord Jesus Christ" [Romans 5:1]. I could see that the moment I believed, while up in the woods, all sense of condemnation had entirely dropped out of my mind; and that from that moment I could not feel a sense of guilt or condemnation by any effort that I could make. My sense of guilt was gone; my sins were gone; and I do not think I felt any more sense of guilt than if I never had sinned. (Edman)

This story reminds me of what must have happened to Jacob in Genesis 32: 22-32, as he wrestled with God and wouldn't let go until he received the blessing. In the same way, Finney hung on to God until he received his blessing—forgiveness, cleansing and the baptism of the Holy Spirit. He was a man anointed with God's power and enabled to walk in God's preordained path for him. He could do this because he had humbled himself before a mighty God and could hear God's voice in the inner man. Charles Finney had moved with his life to a hearing place.

Recommended Reading

Baird & Collins, *Protestantism in Italy & the Waldenses*, 1847

Billhermer, *Destined for the Throne*, CLC

Blair & Hunt, *The Korean Pentecost, Banner of Truth*, 1977

Bonar, *Memoirs & Remains of R. M. M'Cheyne, Middleton*, 1854

Bonner, *Brokenness, the Forgotten Factor of Prayer*

Bonner, *What's Wrong With America—Satan's Attack on the Home*

Bonner, *God Can Heal Your Mind*

Bonner, *Spiritual Warfare Prayer Study Guide*

Brown, *Revival Addresses*, Morgan and Scott, 1922

Campbell, *The Lewis Awakening 1949-53*, Faith Mission, 1954

Carvosso, *The Life of William Carvosso*, Jennings & Pye, 2nd ed., 1835

Chambers, Oswald, *My Utmost for His Highest*, CLC

Culpepper, *The Shantung Revival*, Southern Baptist Home Mission Board, 1971

Davies, *Fire on the Mountains*, Zondervan, 1966

Dallimore, *George Whitefield*, 2 vols, Banner of Truth, 1970

Deuwell, *Revival Fire*, Zondervan Publishing, 1995

Diesen, *The Free Church Movement*, Norway, 1957

Edman, *They Found the Secret*, Zondervan Publishing, 1960

Edwards, *A Narrative of Surprising Conversions*, Banner of Truth, 1965

Edwards, *Select Works of Jonathan Edwards*, Banner of Truth

Evans, *Howel Harris Evangelist*, University of Wales Press, 1974

Evans, *The Welsh Revival of 1904*, Evangelical Press, 1969

Evans, *When He is Come*, SMW, 1959

Gillies, *Historical Collections of Accounts of Revival,* Banner of Truth, 1981 (first pub. 1754)

Glasgow Revival Tract Society, *Narratives of Revivals of Religion,* William Collins, 1839

Goforth, *By My Spirit,* Marshall, Morgan and Scott, 1929

Greenfield, *Power from on High,* World Wide Revival Prayer Movement, 1950

Grubb, *Rees Howell, Intercessor,* CLC

Grubb, *Continuous Revival,* CLC

Harris, *Extracts from the Welsh Press,* published privately

Harvey, Edwin & Lillian, *Kneeling We Triumph,* Moody Press

Harvey, Edwin & Lillian, *Royal Insignia,* Moody Press

Haslam, *From Death into Life,* Morgan & Scott

Haslam, *Yet Not I,* Morgan & Scott

Hayden, *Spurgeon on Revival,* Zondervan, 1962

Hession, *My Calvary Road,* CLC

Houghton, *Amy Carmichael of Dohnavur,* 1955

Jones, *India Awake! Thy King has Come,* Sylhet, 1905

Jones, *Rent Heavens,* Pioneer Mission, 1931

Jones, *The King's Champions,* 1968

Kemp, Winnie, *Joseph W. Kemp,* Marshall, Morgan & Scott, 1936

Kivengere, *Revolutionary Love,* CLC & Kingsway, 1985

Koch, *The Revival in Indonesia,* Evangelization Publishers, 1970

Lacy, *Revivals in the Midst of the Years,* John Knox Press, 1943

Lees, *Drunk Before Dawn,* OMF, 1979

Lloyd-Jones, *Revival—Can We Make it Happen?,* Marshall Pickering, 1986

Luther, *A Simple Way to Pray for a Good Friend,* 1585 (In a booklet by Walter Trobish published by InterVarsity Press)

Lyall, *God Reigns in China,* Hodder & Stoughton, 1985

Macaulay, *The Burning Bush in Carloway*, Carloway Free Church, Lewis

Morod, *The Korean Revival*, Hodder & Stoughton, 1969

Mueller, George, *The Autobiography of George Mueller*, Whitaker House

Mueller, *Answers to Prayer: Secrets of Intercession*

Mueller, *God Answers Prayer*

Murray, *Jonathan Edwards*, Banner of Truth, 1982

Murray, Andrew, *Abide in Christ*, CLC

Murray, Andrew, *Absolute Surrender*, CLC

Moody-Stuart, *Brownlow North*, Banner of Truth, 1961

Monod, *The Korean Revival*, Hodder & Stoughton 1969

Nee, *The Latent Power of the Soul*, CLC

Nee, *Normal Christianity*, CLC

Orr, *Evangelical Awakenings in Eastern Asia*, Bethany Fell Inc., 1975

Orr, *The Eager Feet*, Moody Press 1975

Orr, *The Flaming Tongue*, Moody Press, 1973

Orr, *The Second Evangelical Awakening*, Marshall, Morgan & Scott, 1949

Page, *David Brainerd*, Patridge & Co (modern - Edwards, *The life of David Brainerd*, Baker, 1978)

Paisley, *The 'Fifty Nine' Revival*, Martyrs' Memorial Free Presbyterian Church 1958

Penn-Lewis, *War on the Saints*, Unabridged, Thome E Lowe LTD 1973

Rajamani & Kinnear, *Monsoon Daybreak*, Open Books, 1971

Ritchie, *Floods upon the Dry Ground*, 1980

Robe, *When the Wind Blows*, Ambassador Productions Ltd, 1985

Smith, *Beyond the Vail*, Regal, 1997

Sprague, *Lectures on Revivals of Religion*, Banner of Truth, 1959 (first published 1832)

Spurgeon, *Sermons on Revival*, Kelvedon ed. Thornbury,

God Sent Revival, Evangelical Press, 1977
Steer, *Spiritual Secrets of George Meuller*
Told, *The Life of Silas Told*, Epworth, 1954
Tozier, *The Knowledge of the Holy*, Harper and Row
Vulliamy, *John Wesley*, Geoffrey Bles, 1931
Wallis, *In the Day of Thy Power*, CLC, 1956
Westminster Conference, *Preaching & Revival*, 1984
Whitefield, *Whitefield's Journals*, Banner of Truth, 1960
Woolsey, *Duncan Campbell*, Hodder & Soughton, 1974

Epilogue

On June 5, 1997, evangelist Mickey Bonner died while preaching on the power of prayer and brokenness to Bill Gothard's Advanced Training Institute, held in Knoxville, Tennessee. As he was finishing his sermon, Mickey's last words were, "We must learn to pray with the mind of Christ and it will only come when we humble ourselves before Him. It will only come when we are broken." With no sign of pain, the Lord instantly took our brother home before 16,000 people. The assistant safety director at the conference described it well, "He went out in a flame of glory preaching God's Word."

This volume, *Hearing God's Voice from Within*, was finished the night before he heard God's call to come home.

The following quote was taken from Mickey Bonner's book, *Brokenness, The Forgotten Factor of Prayer.*

Robert Murray McCheyne was a godly young minister with a heart for revival. He had organized over thirty prayer meetings in his large parish in Perth, Northern Scotland. He wrote: "I charge you, be clothed with humility. Let Christ increase; let man decrease. This is my constant prayer for myself and you." . . . [B]ecause of ill health, he was sent by the Synod of the Church of Scotland with a party of other ministers to search out the condition of the Jews abroad. "I sometimes think," he said, "that a great blessing may come to my people in my absence. Often God does not bless us when we are in the midst of our labors, lest we shall say, my hand and my eloquence have done it. *He removes us into silence* and then pours down a blessing so that there is no room to receive it; so that all that see it cry out, It is the Lord." . . .one person can bring revival. Historically, every great move of God began in the heart of one broken person in prayer.

Mickey Bonner had prayed for, personally sought, taught about and encouraged individual and corporate revival in the church for over twenty-five years. Now that God has "removed him into silence," we pray that the Lord will "pour down revival blessing so that there is no room to receive it." To God alone be the glory.

In These Desperate Final Days of History
The Church Has Lost Its Power to Stop Satan's Onslaught.
There is But One Hope Left...

BROKENNESS,
the Forgotten Factor
of Prayer

This book will help to open the door to a new and wondrous place in Christ. Don't run from your troubles. Learn to stand in them in praise. Allow God to finish His work in you. Brokenness is the beginning of all true ministry in your life.

May God bless this wonderful volume. It comes from the heart of a man who experienced true brokenness. My prayer is that God will use this book to break our hearts and to bless our lives.
**—Adrian Rogers Pastor of Bellevue Baptist Church
Love Worth Finding Ministries Memphis Tennessee**

This book has all the ingredients needed to assist in sparking a national revival that could spread throughout the four corners of the earth, one person at a time.
It has often been said that true ministry begins with brokenness and the Father has promised that He would not despise the one who is broken. Almighty God is calling everyone to enter into a life-style of brokenness.
—Coach Bill McCartney - Founder/CEO - Promise Keepers

Jesus said, "Blessed are the poor in spirit for theirs is the kingdom of Heaven." The phrase "poor in spirit" means to be broken before the Lord. King David wrote, "A broken and a contrite heart, O God, thou wilt not despise."
The only way to reach God's highest purpose for your life is through brokenness. Mickey Bonner has captured that message in this book. You will enjoy it!
—John Hagee, Pastor - Cornerstone Church, San Antonio, Texas

Good work Mickey. Calvary Road helped, and this deepens the message.
**—Dr. Bailey Smith - Former Pres. of the SBC/
Real Evangelism, Atlanta, Georgia**

**To order this book by Dr. Mickey Bonner,
for information on quantity prices, or for more information,
Please Call 800-365-7729, Fax 281-580-0175.**

Other Materials By Dr. Mickey Bonner

The Force That Moves the Hand of God
(Video/Cassette)

This is a powerful message for all Christians on prayer. Dr. Bonner teaches us how to pray with the mind Christ. This was Dr. Bonner's final message presented to 16,000 people at Bill Gothard's annual home schoolers' conference.

Spiritual Warfare Prayer Study Guide

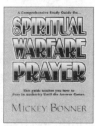

A comprehensive study guide that will teach you how to pray in authority until the answer comes. **Topics Include:** Prayer Is Binding Satan, All Prayer Is Warfare, Conducting Warfare Prayer, Know Your Enemy, The Five U's of Unanswered Prayer, and Prayer: a Weapon in the Hands of God.

Prayer is Warfare

This book brings to light one of the most important principles of prayer—the conducting of warfare against satan.

What's Wrong With America?

Satan's Attack on the Home. The problem in America is the problem in the home! This book will biblically explain how to establish a Christian home.

To order these materials by Dr. Mickey Bonner, for information on quantity prices, or for more information, Please Call 800-365-7729, Fax 281-580-0175.

Other Materials By Dr. Mickey Bonner

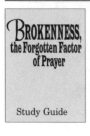

Brokenness, the Forgotten Factor of Prayer Study Guide

A companion to Brother Bonner's book that will challenge you every step of the way as you study, this often overlooked factor of prayer.

God Can Heal Your Mind

The healing of your mind will come only when you are able to face the dark areas and experiences of your life, and forgive. Learn how to bring every thought into captivity to the obedience of Christ. This book has been used mightily in deliverance. (II Corinthians 10:3-5)

God's Answer to the Critical Christian
KYMS - keep your mouth shut!

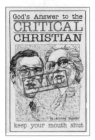

One of the greatest areas of conflict in the human life is negative confession. What we say causes us to be separated from God. This book brings to the reader the Scriptural position concerning their own conversation.

Spiritual Warfare Manual

A "how to" book to equip the Christian in Spiritual Warfare.
Questions are answered:
- How to Break Genetic Ties.
- How to Pull Down Strongholds.
- How to Begin a Ministry of Deliverance Praying.

To order these materials by Dr. Mickey Bonner, for information on quantity prices, or for more information, Please Call 800-365-7729, Fax 281-580-0175.

Other Materials By Dr. Mickey Bonner

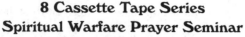

8 Cassette Tape Series
Spiritual Warfare Prayer Seminar

8 Tapes that are a companion to the Spiritual Warfare Prayer Study Guide, teaching the Christian how to pray in spiritual warfare. Among other topics, it includes teaching on Games, Toys, Rock Music, and the setting up of Prayer Assault Teams.

Also Available on Video

8 Cassette Tape Series
Prayer is Warfare

This series was developed to point the Christian to Power through the person of Christ and how to enter into a more aggressive warfare.

8 Video Tape Series on Brokenness

- The Meaning of True Brokenness
- Why We Are to Pray to Be Broken
- How Brokenness Releases the Inner Man
- Brokenness, the Road from Death to Life
- The Ministry of the Holy Spirit
- Brokenness and Prayer Warfare

5 Video Tape Series on God's Power

- The Power of the Blood
- The Power of the Holy Spirit
- The Power of Prayer
- The Power of Brokenness
- The Power of the Family

5 Video Tape Series on the Home and Family

- The Power of the Family
- The Daddy and His Children
- The Husband—Wife Relationship
- The Wife's Place in the Home
- The Husband's Place in the Home

To order these materials by Dr. Mickey Bonner, for information on quantity prices, or for more information, Please Call 800-365-7729, Fax 281-580-0175.

Other Materials By Dr. Mickey Bonner

Individual Cassette Messages - $6.00 each

Dr Bonner has many individual cassette tapes on the following topics. We have selected just a few of the messages to be listed here. Topics include:

Knowing God's Will for Your Life
Brokenness
Praise and Worship
The Home and Family
Spiritual Warfare and Deliverance
Letting Christ Be Lord
Becoming an Intercessor
Spiritual Gifts
God's Power
Establishing a New Testament Church
The Holy Spirit
Salvation and the Second Coming

Some Selected Titles are:

❏ The Meaning of True Brokenness
❏ Why We Are to Pray to Be Broken
❏ How Brokenness Releases the Inner Man
❏ Brokenness—a Gift from God
❏ Brokenness—the Road from Death to Life
❏ Brokenness—the Beginning of All True Righteousness
❏ The Ministry of the Holy Spirit Is Only through Brokenness
❏ Get off the Streets and Get on Your Knees
❏ How to Live by the Power of God
❏ The Beginning of All True Ministry
❏ Where Is Their God?
❏ Those upon Whom God Will Pour His Spirit
❏ How We Conquer by Failing
❏ Any Old Donkey Will Do
❏ God's Purpose in Our Breaking
❏ How to Test Your Walk with Christ
❏ Job—How God Breaks a Man
❏ What Real Revival Sounds Like
❏ Brokenness and Prayer Warfare
❏ Putting Christ First
❏ Hidden in the Day of the Lord's Anger

❏ Repentance—the Prerequisite to Revival
❏ Who Is God?
❏ How to be Empowered by the Holy Spirit
❏ How to Experience the Love of God
❏ How to Have a Spiritual Mind
❏ Preparing for Ministry
❏ Satan's Attack on the Home
❏ How to Move into Warfare against Satan
❏ How Satan Gains Control through Finances
❏ The Role of Satan in God's Perfect Plan
❏ The Five U's of Unanswered Prayer
❏ The Filling of the Spirit—a Must for Warfare Prayer
❏ The Christian's Power to Overcome the Adversary
❏ How Satan Hinders Prayer in the Christian's Life
❏ Our Power to Break the Snare
❏ Twelve Promises for Those Who Do Warfare Prayer
❏ The Biblical Formula for Prayer Warfare
❏ Why You Cannot Hear from God

To order these cassette tapes, for a catalog with a complete listing of Dr. Mickey Bonner's teaching materials, or for more information,

Please Call 800-365-7729, Fax 281-580-0175.